Contents

Recoding Narratives of Race and Nation

Kobena Mercer

The prolific activity of the black independent film movement stands out as an area of development in contemporary film culture that is unique to Britain in the 1980s. The conference on which this publication is based[1] focussed on three recent products of this activity – *The Passion of Remembrance, Playing Away* and *Handsworth Songs* – to take stock of developments in the black independent film and video sector and unravel the controversies generated by the new wave in black film-making. The conference identified important shifts and changes in conditions of production and reception which have enabled the emergence of a younger generation of black British film-makers and widened the circulation of black films in the public domain. In the process it brought together a range of critical reflections which begin to clarify why 'race' has become the subject and the site of so many controversies in British film-making today.

As an active intervention in the cultural politics of cinema, the starting point was to unpack the contradictory responses to the new black British films. The sheer range of conflicting views and opinions surely indicate that something important is going on. Take the case of *Handsworth Songs* (director John Akomfrah, 1987), Black Audio Film Collective's documentary-essay on the civil disobedience that erupted in reaction to the repressive policing of black communities in London and Birmingham in 1985. On the one hand, the film received critical acclaim, and won many prizes including the presitigious Grierson Award from the British Film Institute. On the other, one reviewer in a black community newspaper, *The Voice*, received the film with the dismissive remark, 'Oh no, not another riot documentary' and in *The Guardian* the film was subject to a serious and fierce intellectual polemic from novelist Salman Rushdie. Whereas the film-makers conceived their experimental approach to the documentary genre as a strategy, 'to find a structure and a form which would allow us the space to deconstruct the hegemonic voices of British television newsreels'[2], Rushdie argued that, on the contrary, 'the trouble is, we aren't told the other stories. What we get is what we know from TV. Blacks as trouble; blacks as victims'.

What is at issue goes beyond a dispute over the merits of one particular film. The contradictory reception of *Handsworth Songs* is but one aspect of the growing debates that have focussed attention on issues of race and ethnicity in film and television during the 80s. Other film-making groups such as Ceddo, Sankofa and Retake have also been at the centre of recent controversies arising out of the cultural politics of black representation. Sankofa's innovative dramatic feature, *The Passion of Remembrance* (director Maureen Blackwood and Isaac Julien, 1986) interlaces a rendition of black family life around its central character, Maggie Baptiste, with a series of fragmented reflections on race, class, gender and sexuality as issues demanding new forms of representation. Yet in pursuit of such forms, the mixture of conventional and avant-garde styles in the film has bewildered audiences and critics, black and white alike. Retake's first feature, *Majdhar* (director Ahmed Jamal, 1984) revolves around a young Asian woman whose 'independence' brings conflicting choices and options and for this

reason the film provoked intense criticism not only within Asian communities here in Britain, but across the front pages of the national press in Pakistan. Ceddo, an Afro-Caribbean workshop based in London, have produced a documentary on the 1985 'riots' – *The People's Account* (director Milton Bryan, 1986) – yet although the film was financed by Channel 4, and scheduled for a slot in the 'People to People' series, it has still not been screened on television, as the Independent Broadcasting Authority has demanded editorial changes which the film-makers regard as tantamount to state censorship – a demand which they have resisted.

These developments have taken place in the independent sector, on the fringes of mainstream film culture; but the controversies are of a piece with the contradictory reception of *My Beautiful Laundrette* (director Stephen Frears, written by Hanif Kureishi, 1985). As a relatively low-budget independent production, partly funded by Channel 4, this film took many by surprise with the unexpected scale of its popularity. Few would have anticipated that a gay romance between a British-born Asian and an ex-National Front supporter, set against the backdrop of Thatcherite enterprise culture, would be the stuff of which box office successes are made! Yet it is precisely this 'crossover' phenomenon – whereby material with apparently marginal subject matter becomes a commercial success in the marketplace – that pinpoints shifts on the part of contemporary audiences.

This trend, underpinning the success of recent black American independent films like Spike Lee's *She's Gotta Have It* and Robert Townsend's *Hollywood Shuffle*, indicates that the market is not defined by a monolithic 'mass' audience, but by a diversity of audiences whose choices and tastes occasionally converge. Horace Ove's *Playing Away* (1987, written by Caryl Phillips) pursued such a 'crossover' strategy, staging a tense but often comic encounter between a black inner-city cricket team and their white counterparts in the English countryside. But the film was summarily dismissed by Barry Norman – presenter of BBC's popular film review programme – who felt that as a black director Ove should confine himself to stories about black experiences. This reveals a rather narrow view of black film-making, and one unfortunately held by many critics: it therefore underscores the need for a more adequate critical framework for the evaluation of black film – the issue motivating Rushdie's polemic and elaborated upon by Julian Henriques' article included in this *Document*.

Criticism entails more than the ability to define or discriminate between bad and good movies. It plays a crucial mediating role between film-makers and audiences that often determines the distribution and circulation of the films as much as their artistic and cultural validation. In respect of this latter role, it is now necessary to re-evaluate traditional criteria for film criticism as, in many instances, these criteria have been based on a narrowly Eurocentric canon. Moreover, in so far as criticism reflects upon the social significance of cinema – as that cultural arena in which, as Ray Durgant once put it, society reflects upon and adjusts its image of itself – the recent controversies and debates around race and ethnicity demand a reconsideration of what we mean when we talk about a specifically 'British' film culture.

In the case of *My Beautiful Laundrette* for example, a critical discourse needs to account for the fact that, despite its success, many people actively disliked the film – and did so for very different reasons. Among the Asian communities, angry reactions focussed on the less than favourable depiction of some of the Asian characters which, when read as emblematic of the community, were seen as reinforcing certain ethnic stereotypes. Norman Stone on the other hand singled out *Laundrette* and *Sammie and Rosie Get Laid* in his appraisal of British cinema, for portraying a 'negative image' of contemporary England. Stone regarded the films as inherently 'disgusting' and symptomatic of the artistic and economic 'sickness' of the British film industry, which he traced to the malignant influence of 'left' intellectuals from the 1930s and 60s. In counterpoint, one example of 'good' British film-making that Stone selected for praise was *A Passage to India* (director David Lean, 1987), an epic adaptation of the literary classic reframed for cinema in what has become known, after the success of television drama such as *Jewel in the Crown* (Granada TV, 1983), as the 'Raj nostalgia mode'[3].

cultural value and national identity are themselves becoming increasingly fractured, fragmented and de-centred.

A consistent thematic concern with contradictory experiences in the formation of black British identity runs throughout black film-making in Britain as a generic characteristic. Far from being a parochial concern, this theme raises questions of representation that speak directly to the experience of cultural fragmentation and displaced selfhood that has become such a general preoccupation in postmodern trends in the arts. Reflecting on 'identity' in a previous ICA Document and on the feeling of displacement entailed by the experience of migration from colonial periphery to post-colonial metropolis, Stuart Hall has commented on the nature of this paradox:

Now that, in the postmodern age, you all feel so dispersed, I become centred. What I've thought of as dispersed and fragmented comes, paradoxically, to be *the* representative modern experience![5]

To the extent that the convergence of concern with identity in postmodernism has been diagnosed as a response to, 'a crisis of cultural authority, specifically of the authority vested in Western European culture and its institutions'[6], black film-making offers a unique set of perspectives on the fluctuation and

A Passage to India David Lean

What is at issue here is not simply that different readers produce contradictory readings of the same cultural texts or that an ethnically diverse society throws up conflicting ideological viewpoints. More fundamentally, this critical exchange highlights the way image-making has become an important arena of cultural contestation – contestation over what it means to be British today; contestation over what Britishness itself means as a national or cultural identity; and contestation over the values that underpin the Britishness of British cinema as a *national* film-culture.

Such issues provide the scope and context of the introductory dossier and conference papers documented here. As a way into the debates it would be worthwhile to draw out the paradox upon which black independent film-making is poised – as this encapsulates some of the reasons for its current resurgence which has been described as, 'the most intellectually and cinematically innovative edge of British cultural politics'[4]. The fact of the matter is that black film-making in Britain is a marginal cultural practice, but as it expands and becomes progressively de-marginalised, its oppositional perspectives reveal that traditional structures of

potential break-up of hierarchical distinctions between 'high' arts and 'popular' culture, between what is valorised as 'universal' and what is dismissed as 'particular', between identities that have been centralised and those which have been marginalised.

Like other expressive and artistic practices that have developed in the midst of that peculiar collision of cultures and histories that constitutes 'black Britain', black independent film is part of a shift registering a new phase in what Hall describes as the 'politics of representation'. As an element in this general process of cultural relativisation, black film-making not only critiques traditional conceptions of Britishness, which have depended on the subordination of 'other' ethnic identities, but calls the very concept of a coherent national identity into question by asserting instead what Colin MacCabe describes as a 'culture of differences'. This introduction outlines the institutional shifts that have contributed to the de-marginalisation of black film; the widening range of aesthetic strategies which this has made possible; and the reconstitution of audiences in relation to the increasingly local and global (rather than 'national') diversification of audiovisual culture.

Historical formation

The public profile of black independent film-making today might give the impression that this is a 'new' area of activity which only began in the 80s. But it did not; film-makers of Asian, African and Caribbean descent, living or born in Britain, have been a part of the black arts movement since the 1960s. The previous 'invisibility' of black film-making reflects instead the structural conditions of marginality which have shaped its development. An indication of just how recently conditions have changed can be gleaned from the fact that *The Passion of Remembrance* and *Handsworth Songs* were the *first* black-directed feature films to begin theatrical exhibition at a West End London venue, a standard *rite-de-passage* in film culture. This shows how far things have come since the mid-70s when Horace Ove's *Pressure* was the first black feature film to be made in Britain, or the early 60s when the very first films by black directors were made by Lionel Ngakane and Lloyd Reckord. But, it also indicates how far conditions have yet to change before black film is regarded as an integral aspect of British cinema. The story of its development so far must be told, as Jim Pines has argued, as a struggle against conditions of 'recurrent institutional and cultural marginalisation'[7].

As an industrialised art-form, film-making involves a complex division of labour and intensive capital investment and funding: the crucial issue for black film-makers therefore has been access to resources for production. 'Independent' film-making is usually taken to refer to production outside the commercial mainstream, which is dominated by multinational capital and the profit motive. Although the term is something of a misnomer, for as James Snead remarks, 'independent' film is often highly *dependent* on funding from public institutions, it could be said that black film-making has been 'independent' by default as the struggle for access has been engaged on both fronts. The commercial marketplace has provided employment for a few individual film-makers, but not a secure environment for black film-making as a cultural movement. Rather, the grant-aided or subsidised sector has provided the context in which black film-making has grown. Yet even here black film-makers have had to struggle to secure their rights to public funding. As a result of this, alongside the general struggle to establish and secure black rights, what has changed in the past decade is the institutional recognition of black people's rights to representation within film-culture.

The 80s have inaugurated shifts in the policy and priorities of cultural institutions in the public sphere and this has helped to widen opportunities for access to production. These changes in the institutional framework of funding have expanded the parameters of the black independent sector and opened up a new phase which contrasts starkly with the conditions under which the pioneering generation of black film-makers worked. The earliest films – *Jemima and Johnny* by Lionel Ngakane and *Ten Bob in Winter* by Lloyd Reckord (both made in 1963) – were produced without the support of public funds. Like Ove's first films, *Baldwin's Nigger* (1969) and *Reggae* (1970), they were largely financed by the film-makers themselves, who often demonstrated entrepreneurial flair by raising money from unlikely sources.

Ove's first feature length film, *Pressure*, marked a turning point in 1974, as it was the first film by a black director to be financed by the British Film Institute. The BFI's production of *A Private Enterprise*, a dramatic feature set in the Asian community co-written by Dillip Hiro in 1975, and *Burning an Illusion* by Menelik Shabazz in 1981, signalled growing institutional recognition of black film-making within the terms of 'multicultural' funding policy. Yet although this recognition drew black film-makers into the remit of the subsidised independent sector, marking an advance from the previous period, the time interval between productions and the comparatively modest budgets of the productions themselves suggest that, even within the terms of 'official' multicultural policies, black film-making remained marginal in relation to the general growth of the independent sector during the 1970s.

Various factors contributed to the shifts of the 80s which, if they can be traced to a single source, occurred outside the institutions of British society in the political events of 1981; 'riots' or 'uprisings', the term varies with your viewpoint. Over and above their immediate causes as a response to new, quasi-military forms of policing in the Thatcherite era, the events had the symbolic effect of marking a break with the consensus politics of multiculturalism and as such announced a new phase of 'crisis-management' in British race-relations. In the wake of 'The Scarman Report', political expediency – the need to be seen to be doing something – was a major aspect of the 'benevolent' gestures of many public institutions, hurriedly redistributing funding to black projects. Politically, the eruption of civil disorder expressed protest at the structural marginalisation of black voices and opinions within the polity and encoded militant demands for *black representation* within public institutions as a basic right. Culturally, this demand generated a veritable renaissance of black creativity – from literature, music and theatre to photography, film and video[8] and in relation to audiovisual media in particular, this surge of activity coincided with the advent of Channel 4, which proved to be crucially important for black film-makers and audiences alike.

It has been said, apropos the economic decline of the British film industry in the post-war period, that 'British cinema is alive and well and living on television' as TV has provided a unique point of entry into the profession for many writers and directors. With its official mandate to encourage innovative forms of programme making, Channel 4 contributed significantly to the expansion of the independent film production sector. The Channel was also mandated to provide for the unmet needs of various 'minority' audiences, and as a new model of public service broadcasting which explicitly recognised the diversity of audiences in a plural society, its brief on 'multicultural' programming aroused high expectations about black representation. Early programmes like *Eastern Eye* and *Black on Black* received enthusiastic welcome from Asian and Caribbean audiences, primarily because they filled some of the gaps – the absence of black images – in the more entrenched tradition of public service which assumed a single, mono-cultural 'national' audience.

However, while Channel 4 brought TV into line with the ethos of multiculturalism, the multicultural consensus was itself being thrown into question by more radical aspects of black politics and its cultural expression in the arts. Criticisms were made of the 'ghettoisation' that circumscribed such 'ethnic minority' slots on Channel 4. Indirectly, this led to the formation of numerous black independent production companies with the aim of delivering alternative films and programmes to television[9]. Similar critiques were voiced by the independent film-makers' lobby and the women's lobby and alongside these the Black Media Workers Association formed in 1982 to campaign for an equal distribution of employment and commissions. The BMWA's objectives shifted from the monitoring role of earlier initiatives such as the Campaign Against Racism in the Media[10] and were oriented towards pragmatic concerns such as ensuring access to independent production.

Channel 4 has since revised its ethnic programming – *Bandung File, Club Mix* and *The Cosby Show* replaced the earlier output after Farrukh Dhondy assumed the position of Commissioning Editor for Multicultural Programmes. For all the criticisms of 'minority broadcasting' (which have come from the right as much as the left), it should be noted that Channel 4 has taken the lead in encouraging television to rethink its attitude to the cultural diversity of its nation-wide audience. The BBC's self-critique – *The Black and White Media Show*[11] – suggests an indication of the extent to which issues of race and black representation have been acknowledged or at least 'accommodated' as part of contemporary television: the title of the programme puns on 'The Black and White Minstrel Show', one of the BBC's most popular light entertainment shows which only ended, after much complaint, in 1978.

At another level, the limits of tokenism were inscribed as a political shift from multicultural to anti-racist policy. In relation to the local state this process was led by the radical Labour administration of the Greater London Council between 1982 and its abolition, as a result of central government legislation, in 1986. Beyond mere expediency, the GLC took up demands for black representation in political decision-making and opened up a new phase of local democracy involving constituencies marginalised from parliamentary politics. At a cultural level, the GLC also inaugurated a new attitude to funding arts activities by regarding them as 'cultural industries' in their own right. Both of these developments proved important for the burgeoning black independent film sector, particularly for the younger generation of film-makers who formed workshops.

By prioritising black cultural initiatives either by direct subsidy or through training and development policies (as well as numerous public festivals and events), the GLC marked a break with the piecemeal and often patronising funding of so-called

The Black and White Minstrel Show BBC TV

'ethnic arts'[12]. Emphasising broadly educational objectives, the GLC's extensive black and Third World film exhibition programmes such as 'Third Eye' in 1983, were also important as they brought a range of new or rarely seen films into public circulation. The 'Third Eye' symposia in 1985 gathered together film-makers from Britain, the US, Africa and the Indian sub-continent to map out an agenda for alternative interventions in production and distribution and highlighted, on the one hand, common experiences of marginalisation, and on the other, the impact of black and Third World feminism on issues of representation[13]. Like the conference on 'Third Cinema: Theories and Practices', held at the Edinburgh Film Festival in 1986, such events have placed black British film-making within an international context and helped to clarify the innovative qualities that differentiate black independent film from the 'first cinema' of the commercial mainstream and the 'second cinema' of individual auteurism[14].

At the same time however, such events have also brought to light important differences within the black British film-making community. In one sense these differences concern the diverse ideological emphases and aesthetic strategies pursued by black film-makers in the 80s; but they are also structural in nature and stem from the different modes of production of workshops and production companies. Independent production companies – which include Anancy Films, Azad Productions, Kuumba Productions, Penumbra Productions and Social Film and Video, for example – operate within the orbit of the television industry and as such compete in the marketplace for commissions and finance for individual productions. Workshops on the other hand – such as Black Audio, Cardiff Film and Video Workshop, Ceddo, Macro, Retake, Star and Sankofa – are grant-aided and operate in the public sector context of subsidised independence. Whereas the former tend to adhere to the professionalised codes of mainstream working practices, often revolving around the individual director or producer, the workshops are committed to 'integrated practice' which entails activity around areas of training, education, developing audience-outreach and networks of alternative distribution and exhibition as much as producing films themselves, often through collectivist working methods. In this respect the workshops have been enabled by a unique trade agreement between ACTT, the film-makers' union, and a range of public institutions including Channel 4 – the Workshop Declaration (established in 1982) – whereby groups involved in such cultural activities and with a minimum of four staff can be accredited or franchised and thus receive financial support.

Arguments have raged over which mode of production offers a greater degree of autonomy and independent decision-making. Production companies may claim that by working within conventional patterns, black film-makers can negotiate a wider potential audience and thus overcome the risk of 'ghettoisation'. Workshops on the other hand have argued that 'integrated practice' makes the development of a distinct black film culture possible, and thus allows black film-makers the space in which to address issues of concern to black audiences as a specific 'community of interest' and the space in which to explore black aesthetics. The debate is by no means resolved. In any case, it should be noted that the arguments are of a piece with the different tendencies within the independent sector generally: the work of an independent director such as Ken Loach contrasts with the more 'oppositional' orientation of the workshop movement which began with groups such as the London Film-Maker's Co-op set up by Malcolm LeGrice and others in the mid-1960s. With regard to the specificity of black film-making however, it is important to recognise that the emergence of workshops has widened the range of issues that black practitioners have been able to take on, bringing questions of audience and distribution into the arena of funding and development. In contrast to previous periods, the structural shifts of the 80s' have diversified the range of ideological and aesthetic options for black independent film practices. It is this qualitative expansion of approaches to representation that informs the intensity of the debates on aesthetics in the contemporary situation.

Displacing the Burden of Representation

Culturally, definitions of 'indpendent cinema' embrace such a variety of specific traditions – from combative documentary in the Third World or counter-informational video newsreels addressing local/regional community audiences, to EuroAmerican 'art' cinema or formalist experimentation, accomodated in rareified art galleries and museums – that its coherence as a classificatory term seems questionable. This is especially so when it comes to black independent

film in Britain as each of these traditions are relevant to the 'hybridised' cultural terrain in which it has evolved. In addition there is another problematic area of definition concerning the use of the term 'black' as a political, rather than racial category. Throughout the 70s' and 80's, the re-articulation of this term as an inclusive political identity based on alliances between Asian, African and Caribbean peoples in a shared struggle against racism, has helped to challenge and displace commonsense assumptions about 'blackness' as a fixed or essential identity.

A grasp of both these areas of contested definition is necessary for an understanding of the cultural struggle around the social production of imagery that black film-making has engaged. In this sense it would be more helpful to emphasise the 'oppositional' aspects of both terms so that rigidly essentialist or normative definitions may be avoided in favour of a relational and contextual conception of black independent film as a kind of counter-practice that contests and critiques the predominant forms in which black subjects become socially visible in different cultural forms of representation. A consistent motivation for black film-makers has been to challenge the predominantly stereotypical forms in which blacks become visible either as 'problems' or 'victims', always as some intractable and unassimilable Other on the margins of British society and its collective consciousness. It is in relation to such dominant imagery that black film-making has brought a political dimension to this arena of cultural practice. And it from this position that adequate consideration can be given to questions such as whether a distinctly *black* visual aesthetic exists or not; whether realism or modernism offers the more appropriate aesthetic strategy; or whether black film can be exhaustively defined as that produced 'by, for, and about' black people. These issues are taken up in detail by the contributions of Judith Williamson and Paul Gilroy, and, from the comparative angle of black American independent film, by James Snead. To begin to clarify what is at stake, it would be relevant to start with the question of stereotyping as this has formed the background against which recent debates have highlighted the complexity of race and ethnicity vis-à-vis the politics of representation.

Through a variety of genres, from dramatic fiction to reportage and documentary, black film-makers have had to contend with the ideological and cultural power of the codes which have determined dominant representations of race. Stereotypes are one product of such audiovisual codes, which shape agreed interpretations of reality in a logic that reproduces and legitimates commonsense assumptions about 'race'. More broadly, in the struggle against the hegemonic forms of racial discourse supported by racial and ethnic stereotypes, black film-practices come up against the master-codes of what Jim Pines describes as the 'official' race-relations narrative. Within the logic of its narrative patterns, blacks tend to be depicted either as the source and cause of social problems – threatening to disrupt moral equilibrium – or as the passive bearers of social problems – victimised into angst-ridden submission or dependency. In either case, such stories encode versions of reality that confirm the ideological precept that 'race' constitutes a 'problem' per se.

From films of the colonial period, such as *Sanders of the River* with its dichotomy of 'good native'/'bad native', to films of the post-war period of mass immigration and settlement such as *Sapphire* or *Flame in the Streets* which narrate racial antagonism in a social realist style, the predominant forms of racial representation in British cinema and television have produced a 'problem-oriented' discourse[15]. In seeking to find a voice and a means of cinematic expression able to challenge and displace the authority of this dominant discourse, black film-making has negotiated a specific, if not unique, set of representational problems that constitute a particularly difficult 'burden of representation'. To evaluate how different filmic strategies have sought to unpack this burden we need to examine the contradictory effects of realism and how this impinges on the cinematic investigation of the contradictory experiences of black British identity.

A cursory overview of black films made in Britain would show the preponderance of a 'documentary realist' aesthetic in both dramatic fiction and documentary films. This emphatic insistence on the 'real' – often expressed as a desire to 'correct' media distortions and 'tell it like it is' – should be understood as the prevailing mode in which a counter-discourse has been constructed against the dominant versions of reality produced by the race-relations master narrative. From a context-oriented point of view the 'reality-effect' so powerfully conveyed by documentaries such as *Step Forward Youth* (director Menelik Shabazz, 1977) and *The People's Account* (Ceddo, 1987) is an important rhetorical element by which the 'authority' of dominant media discourses is disrupted by black counter-discourse. Furthermore, within campaigning or counter-informational documentary such as *Blood Ah Go Run* (Kuumba Productions, 1982) for instance, issues of form are necessarily and justifiably subordinate to the conjunctural imperative to interrupt the dominant racial discourse. Thus it could be argued that the operation of four filmic values within this mode of practice, transparency, immediacy, authority and authenticity – (which are aesthetic principles central to the realist paradigm) – constitute the means of encoding alternative forms of knowledge to 'make sense' of processes and events from a black perspective. In this sense the focal concern with the politicising experiences of black youth in 70s' films demonstrates a counter-reply to the criminalising stereotypes of dominant media discourses which amplified 'moral panics' around race and crime.

Similarly, a film such as *Blacks Britannica* (made in 1979, by an American TV company, WGBH-Boston, but cited here as it is widely read and circulated as a film encoding a black British perspective) interrupts commonsense understandings of race by 'giving voice' to those silenced and marginalised by dominant versions of reality. Like *Riots and Rumours of Riots* (director Imruh Bakari Caesar, 1981), the combination of oral testimony, didactic voice-over and political analysis advanced in the films by black activists and intellectuals, presents an 'alternative definition of the situation' and one that emphasises the historical legacy of imperialism and colonialism as a factor in Britain's recurrent crises of race-relations. The oral histories of black community life in four British cities offered by *Struggles for the Black Community* (director Colin Prescod, 1983 and produced by the Institute of Race Relations) cut across the de-historicising logic of the race-relations narrative which seems to be premissed on a 'profound historical forgetfulness.. a kind of historical amnesia. . . which has overtaken the British people about race and Empire since the 1950s'[16].

In such instances then, documentary realism has had an overdetermined presence in framing black versions of reality: the 'window on the world' aesthetic does not perform the naturalising function which it does in broadcoast news; rather, by encoding versions of reality from black viewpoints, it renders present that which is made absent in the dominant discourses. As a conjunctural intervention, the use of documentary realist conventions empowers the articulation of counter-discourse. Yet as Pines notes, although perspectives coded as 'black' at the level of reference and theme differentiate such work from dominant discourse, at the level of film-form and cinematic expression these films often adhere to the same aesthetic principles as the media discourses whose power and ideological effects they seek to resist. Pointing to the relational nature of this constitutive paradox, Pines argues that

This is also one of the ways in which black films are marked off from other kinds of independent work, because institutionalised 'race-relations' has a marginalising effect structurally and tends to reinforce rather than ameliorate the 'otherness' of the subject – which documentary realism historically and representationally embodies. Within this set of relations, therefore, it has been difficult for black practitioners to evolve a cinematic approach which is unaffected by the determinants of 'race-relations' discourse or which works outside documentary realism.[17]

The contradictory effects this gives rise to can be appreciated mostly in relation to narrative fiction as the aspiration to authenticity or 'objectivity' entailed by realism becomes more problematic when brought to bear on the contradictory *subjective* experiences of black British identity. Narrative closure, the tying up of the threads that make up a fictional text, is regarded as characteristic of cinematic realism; but the symptomatic irresolution of the story told in *Pressure* suggests some of the limitations of documentary realism in the attempt to re-code the race-relations narrative.

The film's central protagonist, a British-born black school leaver, becomes increasingly disillusioned as he realises that racial discrimination prevents him from attaining conventional goals and expectations, such as a career. The youth becomes estranged from his parents, who believed that because he was born in Britain he would have the advantage of being able to 'assimilate' into British society. He drifts into street-corner society and after an encounter with the police, he joins his Caribbean-born brother in a separatist 'Black Power' organisation. The plot describes the politicisation of his identity or rather, a

Pressure Horace Ove

growing awareness of the contradictions inherent in the very idea of a black British identity where, ideologically, society regards the two terms as mutually exclusive.

In presenting this dilemma in dramatic form *Pressure* constructs an important statement, but in the telling, in its mode of enunciation through documentary realism, the linear development of the story recapitulates the themes of 'inter-generational conflict' and 'identity-crisis' established by the epistemology of the classic race-relations narrative. We are left with an angst-ridden black subject, pathologised into a determinate non-identity by his very marginality.

As Pines has argued, the narrative logic in *Pressure* remains within the problem-oriented discourse of both social realist drama and race-relations sociology. Consequently, the dream sequence at the end of the film, when the youth enters a country-mansion and sadistically stabs at the carcass of a pig, and the final scene of a protest march outside a court-house in the rain, evoke not only the impotence or hopelessness of a politicised black identity, but a certain powerlessness on the part of the film itself, as if it cannot find a successful means of escaping from the master codes that circumscribe it. Ove's rendition of a hostage scenario that occured in the mid-70s, *A Hole in Babylon* (BBC, 1979) also conveys a pessimistic view of black protest politics. But the crisis of narrative resolution in *Pressure* should not be attributed to its author; on the contrary it must be read as symptomatic of a heroic, but compromised struggle with the master narrative of race relations discourse.

In subsequent black narrative fiction films we see the development of different modes of story-telling within this problematic of 'identity'. *Burning an*

Illusion, by Menelik Shabazz narrates a black woman's awakening sense of black consciousness as she discards the signs of her colonised self – 'Mills and Boon' novels and a straightened hairstyle – to rediscover her 'roots' and a politicised self-image. While the linear plot and mode of characterisation are similar to *Pressure* (as the central protagonist is taken to embody a general or 'typical' experience), the shift of emphasis from black/white confrontation to gender politics *within* a black community setting displaces the binary polarisation in which black identity is reactively politicised by its 'opposition' to white authority alone. Yet, by the same token, because the woman's transformation is narratively motivated by her boyfriend's encounter with police and then prison, *Illusion* has been criticised for presenting what is really a male-oriented idea of black women's experiences as the female protagonist is at all times *dependent* upon the 'politicising' role of the male character[18].

The elision of specificity in the pursuit of 'authenticity' within documentary realism also affects Retake's first feature film, *Majdhar* ('mid-stream'). The story concerns a young woman brought to England from Pakistan by her husband, who then abandons her and thus throws her into a complex set of choices. The protagonists speak with neutral accents, an important aspect of the characterisation and chosen by the film-makers to pre-empt the 'goodness, gracious, me' Asian stereotype. Yet, paradoxically, this seems inadvertently to confirm the 'torn between two cultures' thesis which implies that, for Asian women, independence is synonymous with Western, or in this case English middle-class, culture. What is at stake in each of these films is a struggle to re-tell stories of black British identity, whether set in Asian or Afro-Caribbean contexts, within a code or a language which positions that identity as a 'problem'.

marketing cry – 'The British are coming!' – echoing the patriotic theme of the movie itself. In the same year, in the wake of inner-city riots, the 'put-together' Anglo-nationalism so readily and sordidly invoked in the Falklands War showed how durable the grand-narratives of Empire still are.

The fact is that traditional ideologies of race and nation are not being disengaged gracefully: indeed, the culturalist discourse of the 'new racism' and the sophisticated defence of the ethnicity of Englishness developed by intellectuals of the new right from Enoch Powell to Roger Scruton, demonstrates that the understanding and representation of British history is now a crucial site of cultural contestation. The renewed fascination with the exotic landscapes of the post-colonial periphery – India, Africa, Australia – that features so prominently in mainstream cinema in the 80s', suggests a remythification of the colonial past.

This itself is contradictory as the renewal of a characteristically English discourse of liberalism in films like *Cry Freedom* cannot be collapsed together with the exploitation of these imaginary spaces of the Third World as a backdrop for routine romance and adventure in films like *Out of Africa* and *White Mischief* (sic). As an intervention in this conjuncture of images, the dialogic recoding of race, nation and ethnicity in black British cultural production helps us make 'good sense' out of a bad situation. In the context of the post-riots, post miner's strike, post-welfare state society of the present, the questioning of national identity from the margin interrupts, like a spoke in the wheel, the re-centering of cultural identity in popular culture and populist mobilisations. And it is in this context that the issue of audiences for black film becomes important, because just as antique versions of Englishness are being renovated as a selling point for British cinema on the international market, black British films are also being taken up by diverse audiences.

The enthusiastic reception of black British film at recent conferences and festivals as far afield as New York, Munich and Fort-au-France would confirm Coco Fusco's point that the 'other' is in.[25.] Whether this threatens to re-marginalise it as merely another voguish trend to be itemised on the shopping list of the art-world consumer, or instead opens up new lines of trans-national communication between First and Third Worlds the point is that the increasing diversification of media audiences entails contradictions for the future development of black British film. Given the role of television, and Channel 4 especially, in the ecology of independent production, current debates about the future of broadcasting in the light of cable and satellite technologies and the general re-structuring of the industry, offer two competing models of what diversification means. On the one hand, the de-regulation of the television duopoly emphasises the de-centralisation of media production and delivery and the parallel de-centralisation of markets and audiences. While this may bring a short-term expansion of opportunities for independent film-making, it is widely acknowledged that a non-regulated market-place threatens to squeeze out oppositional film practices. On the other hand,

as Channel 4's successes and failures show, the fragmentation of what was assumed to be a homogenous 'general public' into diverse specialised audiences, offers a model of de-centralisation in which black film-making, along with other forms of oppositional work, can be nurtured.

In either case, the scenario is one in which concepts of 'national' audiovisual culture are undermined by the proliferation of networks of production and distribution at local and global levels. June Givanni emphasises the determining role of distribution in widening the range of audiences for black film and building up an economic flow to ensure the viability of continuing production. The diversification of media products in circulation, including black and Third World films, thus raises the possibility of expanding the circuits of exhibition at local, regional and metropolitan venues which have often been blocked by narrow assumptions about 'minority' audiences. The 'crossover' phenomenon (especially significant in the music industry) suggests that films able to draw in a range of 'minority' audiences are capable of successful economic performance.

In this sense, the future of television as a means of delivering black independent films to audiences is as important as its role in the financing of such work. Alan Fountain points to the contradictions of the current situation, in which the consolidation of black independent production has developed alongside the normalisation of Thatcherism: Ceddo's encounter with the IBA shows how the oppositional aspects of black film culture abutts onto the authoritarian re-regulation of the media. And, amidst these contradictions, the future of subsidised independence is in question. Channel 4's model of diversity has been constructed within a concept of public service, recognising and therefore protecting various 'minority' rights to representation. Similarly, institutions responsible for public funding have retained such a notion of representational democracy where the cultural valorisation of independent production takes precedence over commercial considerations.

Today, the break-down of hierarchical distinctions between 'high culture' – the realm in which state institutions are implicated – and 'low culture' – produced by the interaction of markets and social movements from below – is no longer an abstract issue for academic debate, but a process which is sharpening the contradictions between culture and commerce and the politics of diversity. From the comparative perspective of experiences in the US, where black film-makers have necessarily had to engage with the philosophy of the market to ensure survivability, the uniqueness of British conditions, in which black film-making has developed so extensively, comes into view. The question now, perversely enough, is which parts of our 'national' audiovisual culture do we want to preserve, defend and conserve in the face of the encroaching law of the marketplace?

Kobena Mercer has contributed reviews, reports and articles on black film to *Screen*, *New Socialist* and *Undercut*. He co-ordinated the 'Black Film/British Cinema' conference and is co-editing a forthcoming issue of *Screen*, entitled 'The Last Special Issue on Race'.

[handwritten margin notes: "mythical past", "NB", "antique version of English ers."]

Notes

1 'Black Film/British Cinema', was held on 6 February 1988 at the ICA and sponsored by the Production Division and former Ethnic Advisor of the British Film Institute. The title, incidentally, was derived from a day event organised by Peter Hames at Stoke Regional Film Theatre in November 1987.

2 Reece Auguiste, 'Handsworth Songs: Some background notes', in *Framework*, n35 1988, p 6.

3 See, Salman Rushdie, 'The Raj Revival', *Observer*, April 1984, reprinted in John Twitchin (ed) *The Black and White Media Book*, Trentham Books, 1988, p130: and Farrukh Dhondy, 'Ghandi: Myth and Reality' in *Emergency*, n1, 1984.

4 Paul Willemen, 'The Third Cinema Question: notes and reflections' in *Framework*, n 34, 1987, p 36.

5 Stuart Hall, 'Minimal Selves', in Lisa Appignanesi (ed) *Identity* ICA Documents n 6, 1988, p 44.

6 Craig Owens, 'The Discourse of Others: Feminists and Postmodernism', in Hal Foster (ed) *Postmodern Culture*, Pluto, 1985, p 57.

7 Jim Pines, 'The Cultural Context of Black British Cinema' in Mbye Cham and Claire Andrade-Watkins (eds.) *BlackFrames: Critical Perspectives on Black Independent Cinema*, MIT Press, 1988 p 26. This publication was produced as part of 'Celebration of Black Cinema', a programme featuring a range of black British film, held in Boston, April 1988.

8 An overview of black arts in the 80s is provided by, Kwesi Owusu (ed) *Storms of the Heart: An anthology of Black Arts and Culture*, Camden Press, 1988.

9 For a critique for Channel 4's initial entertainment and current affairs programmes addressed to the Afro-Carribbean communities, see Paul Gilroy, 'Bridgehead or Bantustan?', *Screen* v24, n 4-5, 1983.

10 See, Phil Cohen and Carl Gardner (eds.) *It ain't half racist mum*, Comedia/Campaign Against Racism in the Media, 1982: for reflections on a BBC 'Open Door' programme produced by CARM, see Stuart Hall 'The Whites of their Eyes: Racist Ideologies and the Media', in Bridges and Brunt (eds.) *Silver Linings*, Lawrence and Wishart, 1981.

11 See John Twitchin (ed), *The Black and White Media Book*, op cit. and on Channel 4's minority programmes in relation to the audience, see David Docherty, David Morrison and Michael Tracey, *Keeping Faith? Channel 4 and its Audience*, Broadcasting Research Unit/John Libbey, 1988.

12 Funding policies in relation to the black arts movement are critically examined in Kwesi Owusu, *The Struggle for Black Arts in Britain*, Comedia 1986

13 The event, organised by Parminder Vir and co-ordinated by June Givanni, is documented in *Third Eye: Struggle for Black and Third World Cinema*, GLC Race Equality Unit, 1986.

14 For two conflicting accounts of the event, see my report in *Screen*, v27 n6, 1986 and David Will's report in *Framework* 32/33, 1986. The rather ethnocentric views expressed in the latter are the subject of a counter-reply in Clyde Taylor, 'Eurocentrics vs. New Thought at Edinburgh', *Framework* n 34, 1987. Proceedings from the conference will be published in Jim Pines and Paul Willemen (eds.) *Third Cinema*, British Film Institute (forthcoming).

15 See, Jim Pines, 'Black in Films: The British Angle', in *Multi racial Education* (Special Issue on Race and the Media), v 9 n 2 1981. The analysis of ethnic stereotyping is also discussed by Homi Bhabha in his influential essay, 'The Other Question: The Stereotype and Colonial Discourse', *Screen* v 24, n 4, 1983.

16 Stuart Hall, 'Racism and Reaction', in *Five Views on Multiracial Britain*, Commission for Racial Equality, 1979, p 25; see also, Stuart Hall, 'The Whites of their Eyes', in *Silver Linings*, op cit.

17 'The Cultural Context of Black British Film', in *BlackFrames*, op cit. p29.

18 See Sally Sayers and Layleen Jayamanne, 'Burning an Illusion' in Charlotte Brundson (ed) *Films for Women*, British Film Institute, 1986; see also, Martine Attille and Maureen Blackwood, 'Black Women and Representation' in the same volume.

19 Dick Hebdige, 'Digging for Britain: an excavation in seven parts' in *The British Edge*, Institute of Contemporary Arts, Boston, Mass. 1987.

20 I have drawn on Bahktin's concept of dialogism, developed in *The Dialogic Imagination* (University of Texas, 1981), in my essay, 'Diaspora Culture and the Dialogic Imagination: The Aesthetics of Black Independent Film in Britain', in *BlackFrames*, op cit. See also, on the range of arguments around aesthetics, contributions to *Undercut* n 17 (London Film-Makers Co-op, 1988) from the 'Cultural Identities' conference held at the Commonwealth Institute in March 1986.

21 Bhabha's concept of 'hybridity' is developed in 'Signs Taken for Wonders: Questions of Ambivalence and Authority Under a Tree Outside Delhi, May 1817', in Henry Louis Gates, Jr. (ed), *Race, Writing and Difference*, University of Chicago, 1988. Gilroy's discussion of syncretism and diasporean culture is developed in *There Ain't No Black in the Union Jack*, Hutchinson, 1988 (esp Ch 5, 'Diaspora, Utopia and the critique of capitalism').

22 In Paul Gilroy and Jim Pines, 'Handsworth Songs: Audiences/Aesthetics/Independence', Interview with Black Audio Film Collective, *Framework*, n 35, 1988, p11.

23 In 'The Passion of Remembrance: Background', *Framework* 32/33, p.101, and reprinted here in the dossier.

24 *New Statesman*, 5 December, 1986.

25 See Coco Fusco's report on recent conferences in Boston and New York, 'Fantasies of Oppositionality', in *Screen* – 'The Last 'Special Issue' on Race' (forthcoming, 1988).

Critical Voices: a selection of recent articles

Songs Doesn't Know the Score

Salman Rushdie

In *The Heart of a Woman*, volume four of her famous autobiography, Maya Angelou describes a meeting of the Harlem Writers' Guild, at which she read some of her work and had it torn to pieces by the group.

It taught her a tough lesson: 'If I wanted to write, I had to be willing to develop a kind of concentration found mostly in people awaiting execution. I had to learn technique and surrender my ignorance.'

It just isn't enough to be black and blue, or even black and angry. The message is plain enough in Angelou's self-portrait, in Louise Meriwether's marvellous *Daddy Was A Numbers Runner*, in Toni Morrison and Paule Marshall; if you want to tell the untold stories, if you want to give voice to the voiceless, you've got to find a language. Which goes for film as well as prose, for documentary as well as autobiography. Use the wrong language, and you're dumb and blind.

Down at the Metro cinema, in Soho, there's a new documentary starting a three-week run, *Handsworth Songs*, made by Black Audio Film Collective. The 'buzz' about the picture is good. New Socialist likes it, City Limits likes it, people are calling it multi-layered 'original' imaginative, its makers talk of speaking in metaphors, its director John Akomfrah is getting mentioned around town as a talent to watch.

Unfortunately, it's no good, and the trouble does seem to be one of language.

Let me put it this way. If you say 'Handsworth,' what do you see? Most Britons would see fire, riots, looted shops, young Rastas and helmeted cops by night. A big story; front page. Maybe a West Side Story : Officer Krupke, armed to the teeth versus the kids with the social disease.

There's a line that *Handsworth Song* wants us to learn. 'There are no stories in the riots,' it repeats, 'only the ghosts of other stories'. The trouble is, we aren't told the other stories. What we get is what we know from TV. Blacks as trouble; blacks as victims. Here is a Rasta dodging the police; here are the old news-clips of the folks in the fifties getting off the boat, singing calypsos about 'darling London'.

Little did they know, eh? But we don't hear about their lives, or the lives of their British-born children. We don't hear Handsworth's songs.

Why not? The film's handouts provide a clue. 'The film attempts to excavate hidden ruptures/agonies of "Race".' It 'looks at the riots as a political field coloured by the trajectories of industrial decline and structural crisis.' Oh dear. The sad thing is that while the film-makers are trying to excavate ruptures and work out how trajectories can colour fields, they let us hear so little of the much richer language of their subjects.

When Home Secretary Hurd visits Handsworth looking bemused, just after the riots, a black voice is heard to say: 'The higher monkey climb the more he will expose.' If only more of this sort of wit and freshness could have found its way into the film. But the makers are too busy 're-positioning the convergence of "Race" and "Criminality",' describing a living world in the dead language of race industry professionals. I don't know Handsworth very well, but I do know it's bursting with tales worth telling. Take a look at John Bishton and Derek Reardon's 1984 photo-and-text essay, *Home Front*. There are Vietnamese boat people in Handsworth where Father Peter Diem, a refugee himself, runs a pastoral centre to which they come for comfort.

There's an Asian businessman in Handsworth who made his pile by employing his fellow-Asians in

Handsworth Songs Black Audio Film Collective

sweat-shops to make, of all things, the Harrington jackets beloved of the skinheads who were also, as it happened fond of bashing the odd Paki.

Here are two old British soldiers. One, namely Shri Dalip Singh, sits stiffly in his army tunic, sporting his Africa Star with pride; the other, a certain Jagat Singh, is a broken old gent who has been arrested for drunkenness on these streets over 300 times. Some nights they catch him trying to direct the traffic.

It's a religious place, Handsworth. What was once a Methodist chapel is now one of the many Sikh gurdwaras. Here is the Good News Asian Church, and there you see Rasta groundations, a mosque, Pentecostal halls, and Hindu Jain and Buddhist places of worship. Many of Handsworth's songs are hymns of praise. But there's reggae, too, there are Toasters at blues dances, there are Punjabi *ghazals* and Two Tone bands.

These days, the kids in Handsworth like to dance the Wobble. And some of its denizens dream of distant 'liberations', nurturing, for example, the dark fantasy of Kahlistan.

It's important, I believe, to tell such stories; to say, this is England: *Allahu Akbar* from the minaret of Birmingham mosque, the Ethiopian World Federation which helps Handsworth Rastas 'return' to the land of Ras Tafari. These are English scenes now, English songs.

You won't find them, or anything like them, in *Handsworth Songs*, though for some reason you will see plenty of footage about troubles in Tottenham and Brixton, which is just the sort of blurring you know the Harlem writers would have jumped on, no matter how right-on it looked.

It isn't easy for black voices to be heard. It isn't easy to get it said that the state attacks us, that the police are militarised. It isn't easy to fight back against media stereotypes. As a result, whenever somebody says what we all know, even if they say it clumsily and in jargon, there's a strong desire to cheer, just because they managed to get something said, they managed to get through.

I don't think that's much help myself. That kind of celebration makes us lazy.

Next time, let's start telling those ghost-stories. If we know why the caged bird sings, let's listen to her song.

Song of Handsworth Praise

Sir, I must take issue with the way Salman Rushdie (Agenda, January 12) attacked Black Audio Film Collective and its film *Handsworth Songs*, from his well-deserved but secure position in the literary firmament.

Of course, the film isn't perfect. Of course, a mere recital of the known contours of racism and oppression in the same, old, stale language does no one any good. Of course, black artists deserve something more from us than mere celebration for having managed to say anything at all.

What I don't understand is how anyone watching the film could have missed the struggle which it represents, precisely, to find a new language. The most obvious thing to me about the film is its break with the tired style of the riot-documentary.

For example, the way documentary footage has been retimed, tinted, overprinted so as to formalise and distance it; the narrative interruptions; the highly original and unpredictable sound-track; the 'giving voice' to new subjects; the inter-cutting with the 'ghosts of other stories.'

These new ways of telling bring *Handsworth Songs* into the line with *Passion of Remembrance* and, in a different way, *My Beautiful Laundrette*, in that distinctive wave of new work by third-generation black artists, part of whose originality is precisely that they tell the black experience as an *English* experience.

For what reason, apart from making us look in new ways, does Salman Rushdie want these 'new languages'? He seems to assume that *his* songs are not only different but better, presumably because they don't deal with all that dreary stuff about riots and the police. etc. He prefers colourful stories about experience, closer to 'the richer language of their subjects.'

I fully agree that there is no one 'black experience', and that we need to confront its real diversity without forcing it into simplistic moulds. But subjects and experience don't appear out of thin air. The counterposing of 'experience' to 'politics' is a false and dangerous dichotomy.

Black Audio may have been guilty of mixing its metaphors when it spoke of 'a political field coloured by the trajectories of industrial decline and structural crisis'. But it seems to be struggling harder for a language in which to represent Handsworth as I know it than Salman's lofty, disdainful, and too-complacent 'Oh dear'.
Yours sincerely
Stuart Hall

The Language of Black Culture

Sir, I want to take issue with Stuart Hall's attack (Letters, January 15) on Salman Rushdie's critical piece on the Black Audio collective's film, *Handsworth Songs*.

I write neither from Rushdie's 'well-deserved but secure position in the literary firmament' nor from, dare I say it, Stuart Hall's equally well-deserved but secure position in the academic firmament.

I have been an activist in the black movement for over 20 years, organising and developing political, cultural and artistic thrusts which have emerged from within our black communities and continue to do so today.

For some time now my activist colleagues and I have been moaning in print about the absence of a critical tradition in the field of black arts and culture. We recognise that such an absence is a point of great weakness. Without it we are left with nothing but cheer-leaders on the one hand and a string of abuses on the other.

Realism and the New Language

Julian Henriques

Enter Salman Rushdie with a well-written and thoughtful piece of criticism which serves the dual function of a critique of the film itself, while at the same time laying the foundations of a critical tradition. It is most welcome.

Hall's main objection is that Rushdie misses the fact of the struggle for a new language which the film represents. Rushdie does nothing of the sort. He simply says that the attempt to shape a new language does not work, and I agree with him. In the best critical tradition he goes on to suggest what he thinks would work. And I am certain that the film-makers will take that on board. If they don't then we are in a sorry state indeed.

Finally I could find not a trace of loftiness, disdain nor complacency in Rushdie's critique. His is a useful and timely intervention, a far cry from the patronising 'ten out of ten for struggling' approach.
Yours sincerely
Darcus Howe

Salman Rushdie (India: UK) is the author of acclaimed novels such as *Shame* and *Midnight's Children* and has contributed critical commentary on the arts to *The Observer* and *New Society*. His article on 'Handsworth Songs' elicited responses from Stuart Hall (Jamaica: UK), Professor of Sociology at the Open University and Darcus Howe (Trinidad: UK), former editor of *Race Today* and currently co-editor, with Tariq Ali, of *Bandung File*, Channel Four's black and Third World current affairs programme.

Reproduced with kind permission of *The Guardian*, 12, 15, 19 January 1987.

The current flowering of artistic activity from the black communities is something to celebrate. Whatever the uncertainties of future funding it must be said that across the board, in the visual arts, poetry, writing and performance, black artists are in a stronger position to argue their case and to raise support than they ever have been before. And hopefully it is in such fights that black artists will prove that the roots of their creativity go a lot deeper than recent funding policies.

This position of luxurious abundance in the arts, compared with say five years ago, also raises a number of issues, principal among them is the problem of criticism. *By what criteria should we distinguish between good and bad art?* What do we want art to be anyway? Which developments of style, technique, or content are a step forward and which a step back? In the days when it was an event for a poetry book by a black person to be published, or a play staged, then the struggles that the author had to go through clearly deserved praise – sometimes despite what he or she had actually produced. But now with hundreds of publications, exhibitions and performances available we are in the fortunate position of having a choice as to what we buy and what we go and see.

What makes the choice difficult, I think, is the fact that we have hardly begun to develop any kind of critical framework in which to assess the work now produced. One of the reasons for this, perhaps as a hang-over from earlier days, has been the tendency to rely on a kind of siege mentality which says that anything we do must be good. Also this wishful thinking was made even more destructive when it was applied by members of one political group, no doubt like all the others considering itself *the* vanguard, to anything done by anyone else. Either you were in the group and producing great works, of you were outside and producing rubbish. Such polemics totally destroy any effort to develop artistic criteria through constructive criticism. The result has been very mixed visual arts shows in which the work of extremely accomplished artists is hung next to that of beginners.

The arts institutions have also made their own contribution to the lack of critical debate about black arts. They have tended by stages to ignore totally the black arts; to see them as some kind of exotic marginalia; or to damn them with faint praise. The liberal journalists of *The Guardian, Time Out,* and *City Limits* have done little better with their patronising praise. Like the old story of the black school boy who gets congratulated by his teacher for getting a mark for which a white child would be reprimanded, it's a question of expectations.

The argument of what follows is that the major stumbling block for the development of any black aesthetic or artistic perspective is a general unspoken reliance on a realist tradition. The term 'realism' is generally used to describe the tradition in which works of art are seen as attempting to offer an accurate representation of reality as it is recognised by the viewer. The notion of realism in such diverse works as those of Zola, Courbet and Brecht has of course, been the subject of a huge amount of debate over the years. But I have no intention of taking up any of these issues or even raising the question of what a black realism might be. Rather, I would like to provoke discussion on some of the realist assumptions we tend to take for granted in black art.

One example of what I would call a non-realist work which is worth discussion in some detail, not least because of the amount of controversy it stirred up, is the film *My Beautiful Laundrette*. Directed by Stephen Frears and, apparently more significantly written by Hanif Kureishi, it was first seen at last year's Edinburgh Festival before general release. The film revolves around a gay love affair between Omar (Gordon Warnecke) a young man from a rich and drug-running Pakistani business family and Johnny (Daniel Day-Lewis) an ex-National Front wide boy and their efforts to open 'the Ritz of launderettes' together. Clearly the film breaks quite a few taboos.

Most of the black people and particularly Asians who I have talked to about the film hated it. The reason for this, I think, is because they refused to look at the film in any other way than as a piece of realism, that is to say, a film that attempted an accurate representation of its subject. By that light it failed dismally, according to them. Keith Vaz, the prospective Labour Party candidate in Leicester, in a television interview with Hanif Kureishi put it as follows:

> There were no poor Asians in the film, Asians living on the margins of poverty, which is what we have in this country. The Asian-community was portrayed as being very wealthy, in the best houses (even the father had his own house didn't he?) which is not true. There is mass overcrowding in the inner city areas where the Asian community is.
> *Saturday Review*, BBC2, 16 November 1985

In this realist perspective the film was a failure because it was not true to reality. The critics and the public, on the other hand, appeared to love *Laundrette*. It received rave reviews in such politically diverse magazines as *City Limits* where Mark Finch called it 'last year's best and most audacious comedy' and the *Spectator* who voted it their comedy of the year. Praise from such divergent positions is perhaps cause for suspicion especially when it is coupled with the equally unusual singling out of the film's Asian script-writer as opposed to its English director as the source of brilliance. It's as if the establishment were breathing a huge sigh of relief, saying; 'Phew, at last it's OK to laugh at these wogs.'

In my view the film was a significant success. This is despite that fact that it was not without its racist stereotypes – such as its demeaning portrait of Afro-Caribbean people and 'the Asian woman' with only running-away-from-home on her mind. The success of the film was its break with the realist tradition. The souped-up launderette and the rest of the film were to me a fantasy expressing the feelings, contradictions and imagination of the characters, rather than any attempt to reflect reality. In this light the mother's casting dead mice into a magic potion and the daughter's bearing her bare breasts through the window are nothing to do with what might or might not be actually happen. In fact such events might never occur in reality, but this does not make them any the less real.

What is interesting about *Laundrette* is how it shows the kind of effects that can be achieved once the move is made out of the realist tradition. The film was funny and serious at the same time. To me it was saying something about both the joys and the fears of living in mid-1980s Britain. There are not many films that do that. One that clearly failed in this respect was *Majdhar*. Though with similar Channel 4 low budget finance, comparable themes and actress Rita Wolf in common, *Majdhar* served only to illustrate the crippling weaknesses of realism for coming to terms with contemporary issues. When the film is taken as a transparent medium for the reflection of real social problems very little filmic communication is possible.

Majdhar Retake

Contradiction and Struggle

In contrast the central imaginative leap that a break with realism allows is the possibility of dealing with the issue of contradiction. Generally, the realist tradition assumes an overt link between the presentation and what is represented. That is fine if what is represented is one thing and one thing only. But if reality is contradictory, if we feel different feelings at the same time (funny and serious, for example), if at any one moment we can appreciate opposite forces at work, then the language of realism breaks down. For realism except in its use of irony, parody, etc, a thing cannot be one thing and another thing at the same time. But this is exactly what life is like. *Laundrette* spins round the multiple contradiction of a love affair between two men, two races and two politics.

Besides realism's inadequacy at the descriptive level what the imaginative contradictory world of *Laundrette* points to is the possibility of change. It is only when reality is taken as being full of contradictory tendencies and forces, where at one moment one has the upper hand and at another the other is in the ascendency, that there can be any place for struggle. Once we break with realism's notion that reality is really just one thing that can be more or less adequately represented then criticism and progress become possible.

And the lights of criticism and progress are exactly what's needed in the assessment of artistic production as well as in the political world. In a similar fashion to presenting the conception of a world different from what it seems, realism also restricts discussion of how the world might be represented in art. For realism, artistic judgement always remains at the level of how adequately reality is reflected. The huge assumption that is made in this view is, of course, that we all know and agree what reality is. Though this assumption is hardly borne out by the machinations of black and left politics, it is central to the only kind of criticism that realism can offer. As a result realist criticism is stuck in the 'just like' school: 'Gosh, she was just like my mother ... it's amazing that's exactly how my dad goes on at home ...' Comments like these from the audience as they leave the theatre are the highest praise for the realist playwright.

What prevents the development of any critical appreciation of the work is the idea that because reality is equally apparent to all of us, we are all equally well qualified to judge how well it is represented and how good the artist has been at his or her job. There is simply no need for criticism or the critic. What we get instead is endless discussion about the need for positive images to counter the negative stereotypes we consistently face in the media. The dange of this type of approach is that it denies the role of art altogether. Rather than appreciating works of art as the products of various traditions and techniques with their own distinct language, art and the media are reduced to a brand of political rhetoric.

Clearly steps are already being taken out of realism. In theatre, the most realist of traditions, we can go back to, is Farrukh Dhondy's *The Trojans* for an example of non-realism. In the comparatively new medium of film and video there are more examples notably Isaac Julien's *Territories* and the Black Audio Film Collective's *Signs of Empire*. And there has been, beginning with the publication of *Palace of the Peacock* in 1960, the towering figure of Wilson Harris to inspire us.

Equally clearly, it is not up to me or anybody else to produce dictats on what art and artists should or should not be doing. That is up to the artists to do for themselves in their work and in their manifestoes (it would be good to see more of these too). What we can all do though is to come up with some of the ideas and areas we think worth exploring. I believe this is exactly the kind of thing that should be happening as part of critical and constructive debate. And this is a very important task. If we fail to embark on it we will undoubtedly condemn ourselves at best to repeating other peoples' history and at worst total obscurity. Also, we should remember that a break with realism is not in itself enough. It is what we are breaking *with* more than what we are breaking *from* that is so vital and can give us real strength and real hope.

As an initial move to start the ball rolling, I think we should drop the term 'black' when we are taking about art amongst ourselves. This might appear a shocking suggestion as the term has been hard fought for and has had, and will continue to have, a tremendous polemic value when arguing against the racism of individuals and institutions that refuse to recognise the existence, never mind the value, of black artistic activity. It might have been thought

that these days were numbered, but when over Christmas *The Guardian* can on successive days and weeks publish pages as part of a series 'The Arts in the '80s' and never give one mention to anything black, then that is unfortunately not the case. In this context we cannot afford to be too fussy about the labels they put on us if we decide we really need the resources, airtime or coverage that they have been forced into offering. It is a question of employing the best tactics to exploit the situation for our own purposes.

But now with some expertise in the tactical field we need to turn our attention to what we should be doing with our art practice. We should not allow the particular problems of living in a racist society to cloud our artistic judgement. The slave, like Anancy, has always had to use subterfuge and trickery to survive. With this precedent it's surely not too difficult to have one face for the master and another for ourselves. In my view, the immediate effect of abandoning the label black is emacipatory. Instantly it raises the question: if what we are doing is not black art what is it? As soon as this point comes up we have to begin to make our own definitions.

If we don't make this move the black arts in Britain are likely to become as frozen in their saying-it-like-it-is realism as traditional art forms have been in their exoticism. That is exactly what the establishment would like. I am confident, however, that our history has more in store for us then the museum shelf.

Julian Henriques is an independent director whose films include *Exit No Exit*, a story in dance and music choreographed by Darshan Singh-Buller. A former editor of *Ideology and Consciousness*, Henriques is currently working with the BBC's *Arena* arts programme.

Edited and reprinted, with kind permission, from *Artrage* n13, Summer 1986.

Dirty Linen

Mahmood Jamal on My Beautiful Laundrette

For most of us who cannot afford washing machines or expensive laundry bills, the launderette offers an imperfect but useful alternative. The more sensitive amongst us prefer to wash our dirty linen at home and bring only our less soiled garments into the public gaze. However, those who are in positions of power and control, and can bear the expense of laundries (paid for by their employers), always come out neat and clean. They need no defending even if an occasional stain shows on their otherwise immaculate image.

My Beautiful Laundrette Stephen Frears/Hanif Kureishi

Being constantly misrepresented in the media can make one unbearably sensitive to issues of stereotyping and lead us into protecting and defending every stain that shows up when we wear our badly washed clothes. On the other hand we should not hesitate to challenge those who like to sling mud at us in the name of 'artistic' freedom.

It is quite unfortunate that while Asian film-making is in its infancy in Britain, a film like *My Beautiful Laundrette* should be released to wide public acclaim. Intellectuals who should know better, have been influenced by media hype and box office returns, exhorting other filmmakers to indulge in similar ventures. In some ways the film is an example of what Asian filmmakers should try to avoid: the caricature and the reinforcing of stereotypes of their own people for a few cheap laughs.

The usual answer one gets from people who write or produce such one dimensional dramas is that we are being over-protective and are trying to cover up all the dirt that lies scattered in our community. The other typical response from such quarters is that 'these things do happen in the Asian Community'. Well, almost everything one can think of, from child abuse and rape to drug dealing and murder does happen in every community, but the way these issues are selected and contextualised is what determines whose interest is being serviced. No matter how hard we try, the issue of representation cannot be side-stepped or swept under the carpet.

In this respect, *My Beautiful Laundrette* is an honest film reflecting the author's thinking. It is a state of mind that I can only describe as neo-orientalist. Edward Said in his book, *Orientalism*, described orientalism as a set of attitudes and assumptions through which the Orient was incorporated in western thought by European scholars. Neo-orientalism best describes the way the Asian community is incorporated within contemporary culture by Asian intellectuals who have been laundered by the British university system.

The main Asian characters in the film are a young man (gay), his uncle (an adulterer and money-crazed businessman who keeps throwing out poor tenants from his houses), his father (a bedridden alcholic), his cousin (a dope dealer), his uncle's frustrated daughter, and his superstitious wife who makes magic potions. As if all this were not enough, the saving grace of the film comes in the form of an ex-fascist who happens to fall in love with this white-washed Asian boy, a supposed example of what assimilated Pakis should be like viz; as much like their white counterparts as possible. The story is about how this young man drifts through life aided by his white lover whilst constantly being harrassed by his pig of an uncle and embarrassed by his own kind. The only person who makes a moral choice of any serious kind in the film is his gay lover, a white knight in shining armour. The author has unwittingly betrayed a truth; the powerless are not in a position to agonise over moral dilemmas or masturbate over exotic fantasies. What is surprising about the film is that it expresses all the prejudices that this society has felt about Asians and Jews – that they are money grabbing, scheming, sex-crazed people. It's not surprising therefore, that it was popular with European audiences. It says everything they thought about us but were afraid to say.

It goes further. It asks us to understand and at times even sympathise with those poor white unemployed youngsters who hang around menacingly and bash up the Pakis, who after all, are nasty shop-keepers and dope dealers anyway! It is not as some critics have described it, a view of Thatcher's Britain. To me it is a view of Britain as it has always been, seen through the rose tinted spectacles of a liberal offering love between two individuals as a solution to historically based social contradictions, a solution which does not take us into account. Apart from all the other issues, this, to me, is the film's greatest weakness. The soggy liberalism that seems to hang out of the door of the washing machine, the underclothing left by someone too timid to arouse attention to himself by daring to move it and sling it in the dryer of harsh reality.

As in other areas of cultural expression, Asian filmmakers and writers are now basically divided into two opposing camps. There are those who have taken it upon themselves to present Asians as objects of entertainment and ridicule – anxious to make us more acceptable to British audiences by making them laugh (and us less threatening), and there are others who see their task as reducing the imbalance caused by decades of misrepresentation and stereotyping that we have suffered at the hands of the media in general. Both these groups have a tendency to indulge in rhetoric and one dimensionality which results in the loss of artistic merit in their work. But those who ridicule us are seen by liberal critics as doing a good job, as being broad minded and self-critical, no matter how superficial or absurd their perception may be. The critics who have praised *My Beautiful Laundrette* are the same ones who will jump on us for using 'anti-racist rhetoric' as soon as we talk of racism. For example, they never consider the fact that humour undermines the powerless and gives strength to the powerful. Jokes at the expense of the dominated, line the pockets of the dominators.

HAM AH BHI KARTE HAIN TO HOJATE HAIN BADNAM WOH QATL BHI KARTE HAIN TO CHAR-CHAR NAHIN HOTA (We only have to sigh and stand condemned. They can go and murder and no-one complains!)

My Beautiful Laundrette's argument is quite simple and dangerous. Those who assimilate are goodies. Those who don't carry and on with their 'dirty habits' are the baddies. It is a view most conservative thinkers, who equate Englishness with British, will gladly advocate and encourage. Well, good luck to them. We have other ideas. To present us as people who can be globalised into some universalising fantasy is not acceptable. Our terms of reference, our starting point is an acknowledgement of difference. Moreover, we believe we live in a divided society. We want to take sides, to turn our satire against the powerful; not to ridicule and undermine the weak, not to dilute our identity to make us more acceptable. If 'British' audiences are not ready for us, we know that Asian audiences here are. In *My Beautiful Laundrette*, the adulterous Pakistani businessman complains to his brother 'The country is being sodomised by religion'. If the choice were ever as stark as being 'sodomised' by religion or by racists, I would certainly opt for religion. It is more dignified.

**Mahmood Jamal, poet and film-maker, is a
founder member of the Retake Film and
Video Workshop based in Camden, London.
Among the films he has produced are
Majdhar (1984) and *Hotel London* (1987).**

Reprinted, with kind permission, from *Artrage*, n17, Autumn 1987.

Through a Lens Darkly

Norman Stone

Time was when the British cinema turned out well-made films, in black and white, which drew (and can still draw) large audiences, and made tolerable sums of money – or at any rate launched some of the participants on the road to Hollywood.

Such films were designed for an intelligent and benevolent audience. They tell stories, sometimes harrowing ones; if they have a 'message', it does not obtrude; they follow the old rules of our theatre, that there should be a beginning, a middle and an end, that you should want to know what happens next, and that the characters are interesting. This tradition marched steadily on into the 1950s – among its great exponents were David Lean, Michael Powell and Carol Reed, whose *Third Man* remains the great British post-war thriller.

And now? I have just seen six very recent films: *Business As Usual, Empire State, Eat The Rich, My Beautiful Laundrette, The Last of England* and *Sammy and Rosie Get Laid.* Each of them has been stamped with approval, and sometimes more than that. Each might have come straight from the agitprop department of the late GLC.

They are all very depressing, and are no doubt meant to be. The rain pours down; skinheads beat people up; there are race riots; there are drug fixes in squalid corners; there is much explicit sex, a surprising amount of it homosexual and sadistic; greed and violence abound; there is grim concrete and much footage of 'urban decay'; on and off there are voice-overs by Mrs Thatcher, Hitler, etc.

Plots are desultory, messy, and in one case non-existent. Endings are melodramas of the corpses-on-the-stage type, revealing that the makers have either run out of money or, more likely, of ideas. A few of the actors make a decent show of keeping these confections together, but wood and ham are otherwise much in evidence.

Somehow, their visual world has been dominated by a left-wing orthodoxy: the done thing is to run down Mrs Thatcher, to assume that capitalism is parasitism, that the established order in this country is imperialist, racist, profiteering, oppressive to women and other minorities.

It raises the question of what is happening to the British film industry that so many of its artefacts are of this kind.

Worthless and insulting as this farrago of films is, it does have roots in an interesting and important tradition. To understand, it, we must go back to the early 1930s, a crucial period of transition when the establishment was all-powerful and in a position to enforce 19th century rules, with all their obvious injustice, in the face of 20th century opportunities.

It was an era that bred disenchantment, as official rhetoric and public reality moved further apart than ever before; the League of Nations was supposed to ensure peace, but when war broke out in 1939, it discussed standardisation of level-crossings; the British empire was supposed to last for ever, but in reality was already becoming so much bankrupt real estate.

In the 1930s the younger generation of the intelligentsia in this country turned firmly to the left.

For the first time, masses of school teachers, critics, and academics took Marxism seriously, shut their eyes to the horrors of Stalinism, and prepared the way for the Labour landslide of 1945.

I do not know what brought about this 'alienation of the intelligentsia'. Was it delayed pacifism? Overproduciton of graduates? Difficulties in employment? A conflict of generations? Whatever the answer, this process shifted our intellectual goalposts away from Kipling and Buchan to Auden and the world view of the Left Book Club, with its ranks of yellow tomes proclaiming this or that evil of capitalism.

But this shift to the left was largely confined to the written word. In film and theatre, there was still an enormous mass audience and its concerns were a long way removed from those of the intellectual elite. True, there was a form of censorship that reflected the self-confident values of the establishment and that intervened even at script level to prevent the undesirable getting onto the screen. However it *was* possible to get round this with documentaries, and in any case I doubt whether the censorship was out of step with what the public wanted. One great feature of the 1930s was that, however vehemently the intelligentsia denounced capitalism, the mass of the people went on voting for a Conservative-dominated national government.

There were horrible pockets of long-term unemployment, but in the English south new industries came up and profited greatly from a movement of labour away from the stricken old industries of the north. In 1939, this country as a whole was only just behind the US in its general level of prosperity, so that our received idea of the 1930s as the 'black decade' needs a certain amount of correction.

The effects of this – a proliferation of small motor cars, 'ribbon development' of brick boxes in the suburbs, Butlins holiday camps, *Picture Post*, and the rise of the salacious tabloid newspaper – did not impress the intelligentsia.

After the war, a Labour victory in 1945 might have heralded the dawn of socialism for the intellectual elite but it made little impact on the entertainment demands of the public as a whole. Cinema audiences of that time – large and enthusiastic, showing no interest at all in left-wing propaganda – demanded, and got, stories, characters, good acting. The world of the Ealing comedies and of the Boulting brothers is really a very innocent, decent place, where regardless of political leanings there is a sense of rightness. It was not until the 1960s that film caught up with the written word of the 1930s and passed into a left-wing phase.

In the 1960s, attacking the establishment became the done thing for British film makers, following the Royal Court theatrical revolution. It was the era of 'kitchen sink' cinema. You could concentrate on the grimness of social surroundings – shotgun weddings in filthy northern towns – or the stupidity and wickedness of the British imperial past, in Joan Littlewood's stage musicial, later a film, *Oh! What a Lovely War.*

A surprising number of the films and plays of that era have survived quite well. *Saturday Night and Sunday Morning* was well crafted and well acted, sometimes very funny. It also managed to be serious without being portentous.

But alongside the quality in some of these films came a new element: sleazy, sick hedonism replaced 1930s-style social criticism, such as the vacuous Beatles films *A Hard Day's Night* and *Help!*. Sensationalism and the urge to shock replaced responsible social comment. Realism, social or otherwise, was excluded. And so we come to their disgusting mid-1980s descendants, the six films I have mentioned.

Theirs is a flat, two-dimensional ideology. Yes, there are nasty patches in modern Britain, and parts of our great cities are a disgrace. And yes, it is right for film makers to be concerned with these bad patches if they can be converted into meaningful film in the long and worthy tradition of social-realist films. But the vision of England they provide has nothing to offer an overwhelming majority of the potential audience. They represent at best a tiny part of modern England, and, more likely, a nasty part of their producers' brains.

Why has this happened? Part of the answer must lie in the economics of the film trade. Television threw the cinema on to the defensive and has turned film makers into an ever smaller minority, addressing a smaller and smaller audience. If you are in film today, you are competing with what you see as capitalism at its most revolting and cruel: the Box.

Advertisers on the Box can afford high fees for camera crews, and this in turn pushes up production costs for everyone just at the time when profits are disappearing. Big money can still be made out of films, but such films will probably be two-dimensional glossies.

Meanwhile, there are supposedly enlightened semi-public bodies with a certain amount of money to spend on 'open culture', regardless of its market. The people involved in this are scared of seeming reactionary, having once been taught by adepts of the Left Book Club or having had, at some stage in their careers, to appeal to left-inclined ministries and bureaucrats.

But money is still in short supply; the film industry needs constant shots in the arm and its morale is correspondingly low. So if you are a film maker, you therefore export the crisis of your own industry and present a public view of your country which everyone else sees as a childish caricature.

It is paranoia bred of isolation from the real market. Semi-educated ambitious mediocrities over-competing in a declining market, suffering from bouts of muddled creativity, waiting in line to catch public or semi-public money while dreaming of revolting sensationalism, are unlikely to produce anything of value, as these six tawdry, ragged, rancidly provincial films demonstrate.

Miraculously, the whole of the British film industry is not like this and we still produce some good, and even very good, films of a traditional kind. *Passage to India, Room With A View* and *Hope and Glory* show what can be done.

So why have I passed over the best and concentrated

on the six awful films described here? Because the people who made them are the promising young directors, the ones who should represent the future of the industry. And this is the really depressing aspect of the whole saga. If this is the best they can produce, we might as well close the cinemas now.

Professor Norman Stone lectures in history at Worcester College, Oxford University

Reprinted with kind permission of *The Sunday Times,* 10 January 1988.

England, bloody England

Hanif Kureishi

England seems to have become a squalid, ugly and uncomfortable place. For some reason I am starting to feel that it is an intolerant, racist, homophobic, narrow-minded authoritarian rathole run by vicious, suburban-minded, materialistic philistines who think democracy is constituted by the selling of a few council houses and shares.

Its government, elected for the third time, has attacked most forms of legitimate opposittion: the trade unions, the newspapers, the BBC, local government, the universities, the welfare state; gay and black organisations have all been weakened and undermined by a government that really only believes in democracy insofar as it supports them. The few areas of freedom and dissent left are contracting fast. There is sporadic opposition and complaint, but it is feeble and ineffective. The Thatcher 'permanent revolution' has been too swift and far-reaching for coherent response.

It is surprising that having succeeded in suppressing so much with barely an effective squeal of protest, this government and its friends on *The Sunday Times* should be bothered with what is left of the British Film Industry, hardly a bastion of critical intelligence and dissent at the best of times. (It is too in need for money for that.) Last week *The Sunday Times* published a long piece headlined Sick Scenes From English Life.

I was delighted to see that two of the six 'sick' films Norman Stone dealt with were directed by Stephen Frears and written by me – *My Beautiful Laundrette* and our new film *Sammy And Rosie Get Laid.* Whenever a right-wing newspaper calls one of our films 'sick' Stephen and I know we must be doing the right thing.

This is the gist of the paper's criticism. Of *My Beautiful Laundrette* Norman Stone says: 'It has humour and farce but they do not match the overall feeling of disgust and decay.' He thinks *Sammy And Rosie Get Laid* deserves a prize for 'general disgustingness'.

He also calls our films 'worthless and insulting' and adds: 'The vision of England they provide had nothing to offer an overwhelming majority of the potential audience.' This is certainly not true of *My Beautiful Laundrette*, which has been seen all over the world, both on TV and in the cinema, and in Thatcherite terms was an overwhelming business success.

Stone accuses us of dwelling on depressing aspects of British Life like 'homosexuals,' 'grim concrete' and 'race riots.' He says: 'The done thing is to run down Mrs Thatcher.'

Now most film directors and writers enjoy being publicly attacked. It makes them think the little things they have to say about love and society are important, that people are listening for once. So it made our day when Stone decided to come out of the closet as a film critic. But the impulse behind Stone's attack, the ruling notion which underpins his view, is that these kinds of things about concrete and homosexuals and race riots should not be said: perhaps they don't matter, or perhaps they are not representative of the progress this government has made.

Similarly, last September *The Sunday Times* wrote a leader in which they complained of Britain's intelligentsia always 'sniping from the sidelines.' I think this is euphemism for being critical. God forbid that any artist should mention unemployment, or racism, or poverty. Like Norman Stone and *The Sunday Times* and Mrs Thatcher, like the obnoxious and arrogant English cricket team, we should all be batting for Britain too. Everyone should bat for Britain or shut up and not say that Britain is a depressing place for millions of people, or that black people don't fight back against the violence, prejudice and discrimination that cold-hearted and wretched British whites inflict on them every day.

total control of information and thought. Writing in 1938 Forster thought that two cheers, not three, were quite enough for democracy: 'One because (democracy) admits variety and two because it permits criticism.'

Britain is such an unpleasant and cruel country to live in at the moment – and the best and most sensible are leaving if they can afford to – because variety and criticism in all their forms, sexual, political and cultural, are being seen as aberrant, as unnecessary, in the paradise of money being established. Creativity, the human imagination, culture itself, which is a live thing or it is nothing, are being stifled.

Playing Away Horace Ové

The films Stone really approves of are *Hope And Glory, Passage to India* and *Room With A View,* all of which are set in the past. The last two are especially interesting choices. (*Hope And Glory* I haven't seen yet.) Both *Passage To India* and *Room With A View* are stories of the over-dressed British abroad, set against ravishing landscapes. They are romanticised escapism, glamourised travesties of novels by the great E M Forster, the sort of meaningless soft-core saccharine confection that Tory ladies and gentlemen think is Art.

It is easy to forget that Forster himself is a formidable part of a tradition of dissent – didn't the old scoundrel love his homesexual friends more than England? – a tradition that includes Dickens, Wilde, Lawrence and Edward Bond, writers – however different to each other – who recognised it as part of their job to say what is not normally said; to show what is forbidden; to reflect seriously on our actual lives, both private and public; and to show us how we live.

Their works, conceived in freedom, written with integrity and fired by the imagination are forms of rebellion against the sickly kitsch Stone holds dear. Their works tell the truth, and the truth seems not to be required now; perhaps one day it will not be allowed.

This government, already authoritarian, is moving, under cover of freedom, towards totalitarianism,

In these dark times such expression of the human spirit are hated – or put in the Theatre Museum.

Roughly, there were 10 years of relative freedom and progess in Britain, from the mid-Sixties to the mid-Seventies. These have been followed by at least 10 years of guilt and puritanism and censoring and prohibiting and outlawing and clamping down. This destruction of our little Prague Spring has led to an atmosphere so foul and muggy with repression and fear and lack of confidence that the monarchy, the public schools, even the Archbishop of Canterbury – the old beloved targets which writers and satirists since the war loved to attack – hardly seem worth a sideswipe now.

They sometimes even seem benign and relatively decent besides the freedoms the poor, beaten-down, self-denying, complacent, half-blind British have allowed to be stolen from right under their runny noses.

Hanif Kureishi has worked extensively in theatre, including The Royal Court. *My Beautiful Laundrette* was his first film script. His subsequent collaboration with director Stephen Frears is documented in script and diary form in *Sammy and Rosie Get Laid*, (Faber and Faber, 1988).

Reprinted with kind permission of *The Guardian,* 22 January 1988.

Black Film
British Cinema:
ICA Conference,
February 1988

New Ethnicities

Stuart Hall

I have centered my remarks on an attempt to identify and characterise a significant shift that has been going on (and is still going on) in black cultural politics. This shift is not definitive, in the sense that there are two clearly discernible phases – one in the past which is now over and the new one which is beginning – which we can neatly counterpose to one another. Rather, they are two phases of the same movement, which constantly overlap and interweave. Both are framed by the same historical conjucture and both are rooted in the politics of anti-racism and the post-war black experience in Britain. Nevertheless I think we can identify two different 'moments' and that the difference between them is significant.

It is difficult to characterise these precisely, but I would say that the first moment was grounded in a particular political and cultural analysis. Politically, this is the moment when the term 'black' was coined as a way of referencing the common experience of racism and marginalization in Britain and came to provide the organizing category of a new politics of resistance, amongst groups and communities with, in fact, very different histories, traditions and ethnic identities. In this moment, politically speaking, 'The Black experience', as a singular and unifying framework based on the building up of identity across ethinic and cultural difference between the different communities, became 'hegemonic' over other ethnic/racial identities – though the latter did not, of course, disappear. Culturally, this analysis formulated itself in terms of a critique of the way blacks were postioned as the unspoken and invisible 'other' of predominantly white aesthetic and cultural discourses.

This analysis was predicated on the marginalisation of the black experience in British culture; not fortuitously occurring at the margins, but placed, positioned at the margins, as the consequence of a set of quite specific political and cultural practices which regulated, governed and 'normalized' the representational and discursive spaces of English society. These formed the conditions of existence of a cultural politics designed to challenge, resist and, where possible, to transform the dominant regimes of representation – first in music and style, later in literary, visual and cinematic forms. In these spaces blacks have typically been the objects, but rarely the subjects, of the practices of representation.

The struggle to come into representation was predicated on a critique of the degree of fetishisation, objectification and negative figuration which are so much a feature of the representation of the black subject. There was a concern not simply with the absence or marginality of the black experience but with its simplification and its stereotypical character.

The cultural politics and strategies which developed around this critique had many facets, but its two principal objects were: first the question of *access* to the rights to representation by black artists and black cultural workers themselves. Secondly the *contestation* of the marginality, the stereotypical quality and the fetishised nature of images of blacks, by the counter-position of a 'positive' black imagery. These strategies were principally addressed to changing what I would call the 'relations of representation'.

I have a distinct sense that in the recent period we are entering a new phase. But we need to be absolutely clear what we mean by a 'new' phase because, as soon as you talk of a new phase, people instantly imagine that what is entailed is the *substitution* of one kind of politics for another. I am quite distinctly *not* talking about a shift in those terms. Politics does not necessarily proceed by way of a set of oppositions and reversals of this kind, though some groups and individuals are anxious to 'stage' the question in this way. The original critique of the predominant relations of race and representation and the politics which developed around it have not and cannot possibly disappear while the conditions which gave rise to it – cultural racism in its Dewesbury form – not only persists but positively flourishes under Thatcherism[1]. There is no sense in which a new phase in black cultural politics could replace the earlier one. Nevertheless it is true that as the struggle moves forward and assumes new forms, it does to some degree *displace*, reorganise and reposition the different cultural strategies in relation to one another. If this can be conceived in terms of the 'burden of representation', I would put the point in this form: that black artists and cultural workers now have to struggle, not on one, but on *two* fronts. The problem is, how to characterise this shift – if indeed, we agree that such a shift has taken or is taking place – and if the language of binary oppositions and substitutions will no longer suffice. The characterisation that I would offer is tentative, proposed in the context of this conference mainly to try and clarify some of the issues involved, rather than to pre-empt them.

The shift is best thought of in terms of a change from a struggle over the relations of representation to a politics of representation itself. It would be useful to separate out such a 'politics of representation' into its different elements. We all now use the word representation, but, as we know, it is an extremely slippery customer. It can be used, on the one hand, simply as another way of talking about how one images a reality that exists 'outside' the means by which things are represented: a conception grounded in a mimetic theory of representation. On the other hand the term can also stand for a very radical displacement of that unproblematic notion of the concept of representation. My own view is that events, relations, structures do have conditions of existence and real effects, outside the sphere of the discursive; but that it is only within the discursive, and subject to its specific conditions, limits and modalities, do they have or can they be constructed within meaning. Thus, while not wanting to expand the territorial claims of the discursive infinitely, how things are represented and the 'machineries' and regimes of representation in a culture do play a *constitutive*, and not merely a reflexive, after-the-event, role. This gives questions of culture and ideology, and the scenarios of representation – subjectivity, identity, politics – a formative, not merely an expressive, place in the constitution of social and political life. I think it is the move towards this second sense of representation which is taking place and which is transforming the politics of representation in black culture.

This is a complex issue. First, it is the effect of a theoretical encounter between black cultural politics and the discourses of a Eurocentric, largely white, critical cultural theory which in recent years, has focussed so much analysis of the politics of representation. This is always an extremely difficult, if not dangerous, encounter. (I think particularly of black people encountering the discourses of post-structuralism, post-modernism, psychoanalysis and feminism). Secondly, it marks what I can only call 'the end of innocence', or the end of the innocent notion of the essential black subject. Here again, the end of the essential black subject is something which people are increasingly debating, but they may not have fully reckoned with its political consequences. What is at issue here is the recognition of the extraordinary diversity of subjective positions, social experiences and cultural identities which compose the category 'black'; that is, the recognition that 'black' is essentially a politically and culturally *constructed* category, which cannot be grounded in a set of fixed trans-cultural or transcendental racial categories and which therefore has no guarantees in Nature. What this brings into play is the recognition of the immense diversity and differentiation of the historical and cultural experience of black subjects. This inevitably entails a weakening or fading of the notion that 'race' or some composite notion of race around the term black will either guarantee the effectivity of any cultural practice or determine in any final sense its aesthetic value.

We should put this as plainly as possible. Films are not necessarily good because black people make them. They are not necessarily 'right-on' by virtue of the fact that they deal with the black experience. Once you enter the politics of the end of the essential black subject you are plunged headlong into the maelstrom of a continuously contingent, unguaranteed, political argument and debate: a critical politics, a politics of criticism. You can no longer conduct black politics through the strategy of a simple set of reversals, putting in the place of the bad old essential white subject, the new essentially good black subject. Now, that formulation may seem to threaten the collapse of an entire political world. Alternatively, it may be greeted with extraordinary relief at the passing away of what at one time seemed to be a necessary fiction. Namely, either that all black people are good or indeed that all black people are *the same*. After all, it is one of the predicates of racism that 'you can't tell the difference because they all look the same'. This does not make it any easier to conceive of how a politics can be constructed which works with and through difference, which is able to build those forms of solidarity and identification which make common struggle and resistance possible but without suppressing the real heterogeneity of interests and identities, and which can effectively draw the political boundary lines without which political contestation is impossible, without fixing those boundaries for eternity. It entails the movement in black politics, from what Gramsci called the 'war of manoeuvre' to the 'war of position' – the struggle around positionalities. But the difficulty of conceptualizing such a politics (and the temptation to slip into a sort of endlessly sliding discursive liberal-pluralism) does not absolve us of the task of developing such a politics.

The end of the essential black subject also entails a recognition that the central issues of race always appear historically in articulation, in a formation, with other categories and divisions and are constantly crossed and recrossed by the categories of class, of gender and ethnicity. (I make a distinction here between race and ethnicity to which I shall return). To me, films like *Territories, Passion of Remembrance, My Beautiful Laundrette* and *Sammy and Rosie Get Laid*, for example, make it perfectly clear that this shift has been engaged; and that the question of the black subject cannot be represented without reference to the dimensions of class, gender, sexuality and ethnicity.

Difference and Contestation

A further consequence of this politics of representation is the slow recognition of the deep ambivalence of identification and desire. We think about identification usually as a simple process, structured around fixed 'selves' which we either are or are not. The play of identity and difference which constructs racism is powered not only by the positioning of blacks as the inferior species but also, and at the same time, by an inexpressible envy and desire; and this is something the recognition of which fundamentally *displaces* many of our hitherto stable political categories, since it implies a process of identification and otherness which is more complex than we had hitherto imagined.

Racism, of course, operates by constructing impassable symbolic boundaries between racially constituted categories, and its typically binary system of representation constantly marks and attempts to fix and naturalize the difference between belongingness and otherness. Along this frontier there arises what Gayatri Spivak calls the 'epistemic violence' of the discourses of the Other – of imperialism, the colonized, orientalism, the exotic, the primitive, the anthropological and the folk-loric[2]. Consequently the discourse of anti-racism had often been founded on a strategy of reversal and inversion, turning the 'Manichean aesthetic' of colonial discourse up-side down. However, as Fanon constantly reminded us the epistemic violence is both outside and inside, and operates by a process of splitting on both sides of the division – in here as well as out here. That is why it is question, not only of 'black-skin, white-skin' but of *'Black-Skin, White Masks'* — the internalisation of the self-as-other. Just as masculinity always constructs femininity as double – simultaneously Madonna and Whore – so racism contructs the black subject: noble savage and violent avenger. And in the doubling, fear and desire double for one another and play across the structures of otherness, complicating its politics.

Recently I've read several articles about the photographic text of Robert Mapplethorpe – especially his inscription of the nude, black male – all written by black critics or cultural practitioners[3]. These essays properly begin by identifying in Mapplethorpe's work the tropes of fetishisation, the fragmentation of the black image and its objectification, as the forms of their appropriation within the white, gay gaze. But, as I read, I know that something else is going on as well in both the production and the reading of those texts. The continuous circling around Mapplethorpe's work is not exhausted by being able to place him as the white fetishistic gay photographer; and this is because it is also marked by the surreptitious return of desire – that deep ambivalence of identification which makes the categories in which we have previously thought and argued about black cultural politics and the black cultural text extremely problematic. This brings to the surface the unwelcome fact that a great deal of black politics, constructed, addressed and developed directly in relation to questions of race and ethnicity, has been predicated on the assumption that the categories of gender and sexuality would stay the same and remain fixed and secured. What the new politics of representation does is to put that into question, crossing the questions of racism irrevocably with questions of sexuality. That is what is so disturbing, finally, to many of our settled political habits about *Passion of Remembrance*. This double fracturing entails a different kind of politics because, as we know, black radical politics has frequently been stabilised around particular conceptions of black masculinity, which are only now being put into question by black women and black gay men. At certain points, black politics has also been underpinned by a deep absence or more typically an evasive silence with reference to class.

Another element inscribed in the new politics of representation has to do with the question of ethnicity. I am familiar with all the dangers of 'ethnicity' as a concept and have written myself about the fact that ethnicity, in the form of a culturally-constructed sense of Englishness and a particularly closed, exclusive and regressive form of English national identity, is one of the core characteristics of British racism today[4]. I am also well aware that the politics of anti-racism has often constructed itself in terms of a contestation of 'multi-ethnicity' or 'multi-culturalism'. On the other hand, as the politics of representation around the black subject shifts, I think we will begin to see a renewed contestation over the meaning of the term 'ethnicity' itself.

If the black subject and black experience are not stabilised by Nature or by some other essential guarantee, then it must be the case that they are constructed historically, culturally, politically – and the concept which refers to this is 'ethnicity'. The term ethnicity acknowledges the place of history, language and culture in the construction of subjectivity and identity, as well as the fact that all discourse is placed, positioned, situated, and all knowledge is contextual. Representation is possible only because enunciation is always produced within codes which have a history, a position within the discursive formations of a particular space and time. The displacement of the 'centred' discourses of the West entails putting in question its universalist character and its transcendental claims to speak for everyone, while being itself everywhere and nowhere. The fact that this grounding of ethnicity in difference was deployed, in the discourse of racism, as a means of disavowing the realities of racism and repression does not mean that we can permit the term to be permanently colonized. That appropriation will have to be contested, the term

disarticulated from its position in the discourse of 'multi-culturalism' and transcoded, just as we previously had to recuperate the term 'black', from its place in a system of negative equivalences. The new politics of representation therefore also sets in motion an ideological contestation around the term, 'ethnicity'. But in order to pursue that movement further, we will have to retheorize the concept of *difference*.

It seems to me that, in the various practices and discourses of black cultural production, we are beginning to see constructions of just such a new conception of ethnicity: a new cultural politics which engages rather than supresses *difference* and which depends, in part, on the cultural construction of new ethnic identities. Difference, like representation, is also a slippery, and therefore, contested concept. There is the 'difference' which makes a radical and unbridgeable separation: and there is a 'difference' which is positional, conditional and conjunctural, closer to Derrida's notion of *differance*, though if we are concerned to maintain a politics it cannot be defined exclusively in terms of an infinite sliding of the signifier. We still have a great deal of work to do to *decouple* ethnicity, as it functions in the dominant discourse, from its equivalence with nationalism, imperialism, racism and the state, which are the points of attachment around which a distinctive British or, more accurately, English ethnicity have been constructed. Nevertheless, I think such a project is not only possible but necessary. Indeed, this decoupling of ethnicity from the violence of the state is implicit in some of the new forms of cultural practice that are going on in films like *Passion* and *Handsworth Songs*. We are beginning to think about how to represent a non-coercive and a more diverse conception of ethnicity, to set against the embattled, hegemonic conception of 'Englishness' which, under Thatcherism, stabilizes so much of the dominant political and cultural discourses, and which, because it is hegemonic, does not represent itself as an ethnicity at all.

This marks a real shift in the point of contestation, since it is no longer only between antiracism and multiculturalism but *inside* the notion of ethnicity itself. What is involved is the splitting of the notion of ethnicity between, on the one hand the dominant notion which connects it to nation and 'race' and on the other hand what I think is the beginning of a positive conception of the ethnicity of the margins, of the periphery. That is to say, a recognition that we all speak from a particular place, out of a particular history, out of a particular experience, a particular culture, without being contained by that position as 'ethnic artists' or film-makers. We are all, in that sense, *ethnically* located and our ethnic identities are crucial to our subjective sense of who we are. But this is also a recognition that this a not an ethnicity which is doomed to survive, as Englishness was, only by marginalising, dispossessing, displacing and forgetting other ethnicities. This precisely is the politics of ethnicity predicted on difference and diversity.

The final point which I think is entailed in this new politics of representation has to do with an awareness of the black experience as a *diaspora* experience, and the consequences which this carries

Dreaming Rivers Martina Attille

for the process of unsettling, recombination, hybridization and 'cut-and-mix' – in short, the process of cultural *diaspora-ization* (to coin an ugly term) which it implies. In the case of the young black British films and film-makers under discussion, the diaspora experience is certainly profoundly fed and nourished by, for example, the emergence of Third World cinema; by the African experience; the connection with Afro-Caribbean experience; and the deep inheritance of complex systems of representation and aesthetic traditions from Asian and African culture. But, in spite of these rich cultural 'roots', the new cultural politics is operating on new and quite distinct ground – specifically, contestation over what it means to be 'British'. The relation of this cultural politics to the past; to its different 'roots' is profound, but complex. It cannot be simple or unmediated. It is (as a film like *Dreaming Rivers* reminds us) complexly mediated and transformed by memory, fantasy and desire. Or, as even an explicitly political film like *Handsworth Songs* clearly suggests, the relation is inter-textual – mediated, through a variety of other 'texts'. There can, therefore, be no simple 'return' or 'recovery' of the ancestral past which is not re-experienced through the categories of the present: no base for creative enunciation in a simple reproduction of traditional forms which are not transformed by the technologies and the identities of the present. This is something that was signalled as early as a film like *Blacks Britannica* and as recently as Paul Gilroy's important book, *There Ain't No Black in the Union Jack*[5]. Fifteen years ago we didn't care, or at least I didn't care, whether there was any black in the Union Jack. Now not only do we care, we *must*.

This last point suggests that we are also approaching what I would call the end of a certain critical innocence in black cultural politics. And here, it might be appropriate to refer, glancingly, to the debate between Salman Rushdie and myself in *The Guardian* some months ago. The debate was not about whether *Handsworth Songs* or *The Passion of Remembrance* were great films or not, because, in the light of what I have said, once you enter this

particular problematic, the question of what good films are, which parts of them are good and why, is open to the politics of criticism. Once you abandon essential categories, there is no place to go apart from the politics of criticism and to enter the politics of criticism in black culture is to grow up, to leave the age of critical innocence.

It was not Salman Rushdie's particular judgement that I was contesting, so much as the mode in which he addressed them. He seemed to me to be addressing the films as if from the stable, well-established critical criteria of a *Guardian* reviewer. I was trying perhaps unsuccessfully, to say that I thought this an inadequate basis for a political criticism and one which overlooked precisely the signs of innovation, and the constraints, under which these film-makers were operating. It is difficult to define what an alternative mode of address would be. I certainly didn't want Salman Rushdie to say he thought the films were good because they were black. But I also didn't want him to say that he thought they weren't good because 'we creative artists all know what good films are', since I no longer believe we can resolve the questions of aesthetic value by the use of these transcendental, canonical cultural categories. I think there *is* another position, one which locates itself *inside* a continuous struggle and politics around black representation, but which then is able to open up a continuous critical discourse about themes, about the forms of representation, the subjects of representation, above all, the regimes of representation. I thought it was important, at that point, to intervene to try and get that mode of critical address right, in relation to the new black film-making. It is extremely tricky, as I know, because as it happens, in intervening, I got the mode of address wrong too! I failed to communicate the fact that, in relation to his *Guardian* article I thought Salman was hopelessly wrong about *Handsworth Songs*, which does not in any way diminish my judgement about the stature of *Midnight's Children*. I regret that I couldn't get it right, exactly, because the politics of criticism has to be able to get both things right.

Such a politics of criticism has to be able to say (just to give one example) why *My Beautiful Laundrette* is one of the most riveting and important films produced by a black writer in recent years and precisely for the reason that made it so controversial: its refusal to represent the black experience in Britain as monolithic, self-contained, sexually stabilized and always 'right-on' – in a word, always and only 'positive', or what Hanif Kureishi has called, 'cheering fictions': 'the writer as public relations officer, as hired liar. If there is to be a serious attempt to understand Britain today, with its mix of races and colours, its hysteria and despair, then, writing about it has to be complex. It can't apologise or idealize. It can't sentimentalize and it can't represent only one group as having a monopoly on virtue'[6]. *Laundrette* is important particularly in terms of its control, of knowing what it is doing, as the text crosses those frontiers between gender, race, ethnicity, sexuality and class. *Sammy and Rosie* is also a bold and adventurous film, though in some ways less coherent, not so sure of where it is going, overdriven by an almost uncontrollable, cool anger. One needs to be able to offer that as a critical judgment and to argue it through, to have one's mind changed, without undermining one's essential commitment to the project of the politics of black representation.

Professor Stuart Hall is best known for his formative influence on the British left and as the former Director of the Centre for Contemporary Cultural Studies at Birmingham University. He has, in addition, written and broadcast on issues of race, culture and ethnicity, from *The Young Englanders* (NCCI, 1967) to *Policing the Crisis* (Macmillan, 1979). A collection of his essays on cultural politics, *Reproducing Ideologies*, will be published later this year.

1 The Yorkshire town of Dewesbury became the focus of national attention when white parents withdrew their children from a local school with predominantly Asian pupils, on the grounds that 'English' culture was no longer taught on the curriculum. The contestation of multicultural education from the right also underpinned the controversies around Bradford headmaster Ray Honeyford. See, Paul Gordon, 'The New Right, race and education'; *Race and Class*, Vol XXIX, n3, Winter 1987.

2 Gayatri C. Spivak, *In Other Worlds: Essays in Cultural Politics*, Methuen 1987.

3 Kobena Mercer 'Imaging the Black Man's Sex' in Patricia Holland et al (eds) *Photography/Politics:Two*, Comedia/Methuen, 1987 and various articles in *Ten.8* n22 1986, an issue on 'Black Experiences' edited by David A Bailey.

4 Stuart Hall, 'Racism and Reaction' in *Five Views on Multi-Racial Britain*, Commission for Racial Equality, 1978.

5 Paul Gilroy, *There Ain't No Black in the Union Jack; The cultural politics of race and nation*, Hutchinson 1988.

6 Hanif Kureishi, 'Dirty Washing', *Time Out*, 14-20 November 1985.

Black Film in 80s' Britain

Colin MacCabe

I want to start by agreeing with Stuart Hall that the crucial cultural struggle in which we are engaged is the definition of what we mean by 'British'. Small as it is, current black British cinema is at the forefront of that struggle within what one might call, and all the problems are there in the term itself, our national culture. To work in the grant-aided sector over the last five years has been particularly challenging and exciting because it is largely that area which has fostered the first wave of black British cinema. It is that context which provides both my own personal interest and commitment to the themes of this conference and the very fact of the conference itself.

While re-watching films for this weekend, I was struck by the clip of Thatcher in *Handsworth Songs* when she talks about being 'swamped'. It seemed to me that she enunciated very clearly a standard view of integration. On that view, you start with a basic cultural identity and any newcomers must integrate, be absorbed into that identity. If there are too many newcomers then a problem arises because that identity is put at risk. In seeking to oppose the racism inherent in Thatcher's remarks, it is not enough to simply deny what she says. To argue that the cultural identity of Britain is not being put at risk by the immigration of the post-war years is to seek to minimise and maginalise the cultural changes brought about by that immigration. Rather one should emphasize the possibilities and hopes offered by that immigration, above all by the transformations of notions of national and cultural identity that it promises.

For over 400 years we have we have lived with a notion of the national culture as homogenous which presented the simple choice of identification or exclusion. The identity offered has been defined racially in terms of whiteness, sexually in terms of a very limited vision of masculinity and culturally in relation to certain approved forms of speech and manners marked by a very definite notion of English (and specifically not Irish or Welsh or Scottish). There is no better example of this process than Shakespeare's plays. If tragedies like *Othello* and romances like *The Tempest* make clear how crucial are notions of race to the notion of identity, it is the history plays which make clear that the English national identity is to be found in the rigourous subordination of the Irish, Welsh and Scottish. What is exciting and liberating about the potential of black British cinema (and black British culture more widely) is not simply that it challenges that homogenous and restrictive culture but that it challenges, in terms of a very different understanding, what culture might be. It is not, and here I am in complete agreement with Stuart, promoting a black identity which would replace that offered as white, but challenging that very notion of identity. It is a commitment to a heterogenous culture which would embrace difference rather than identity. It seems to me that the theoretical and practical question of how we construct and understand such a culture of differences is crucial for us both locally in Britain but also internationally and indeed I doubt whether those two aspects can be disentangled.

Black cultural workers in general and black film makers in particular face this problem both practically and theoretically at every step – the problem is an integral part of everything that they do. When I saw last year the three films which were the occasion for this conference: *Playing Away, Passion of Remembrance* and *Handsworth Songs*, I was struck very forcibly how they all participated in this crucial contemporary debate about what it means to be British. All three of them seemed to me to reject any notion of an essential answer to this question and to celebrate the production of a culture of differences. This celebration was not a theoretical desire that such a culture should exist but a practical demonstration that it did. For that reason I was rather dismayed by the debates both public and private that they provoked. I heard very few voices congratulating the film-makers for the enormous achievement that these films marked, instead one largely heard them condemned in terms of completely outdated aesthetics. In a funny way, however, those outdated aesthetics informed the films themselves and marked the most important criticism that needed to be made of those films if they were to be used as stepping stones to further and better efforts.

Those who wanted to condemn *Handsworth Songs* and *Passion of Remembrance* argued that they were irredeemably elitist, over-politicised and did not speak to an audience of ordinary people. Those who attacked *Playing Away* argued that did not produce any real political analysis of the social situation but contented itself with stereotypes and a conventional narrative. In fact these debates reproduced, almost exactly a very ancient debate between modernism and realism which found its most important expression in the debate between Lukacs and Brecht in the thirties. If the insights of psychoanalysis were added in the seventies, the conceptions of politics and society were still caught within throroughly Eurocentric modes. And yet this ancient debate does in fact set many of the terms of the film texts themselves. *Playing Away* is couched within a tradition of realism which assumes that there is a general audience, which the work of art can speak to directly, *Handsworth Songs* and *Passion of Remembrance* propose an ideal Brechtian audience, ready to be awakened into dialectical awareness.

Expeditions Black Audio Film Collective

I would argue that both ignore the audiences that they actually address and, in so doing, fail to live up to their true potential. Those actual audiences are best defined in terms of the television slots they were commissioned by – Film on 4 and the Eleventh Hour both on Channel 4. In both cases the audience is smaller but more aware than the audience implied

in the films. To come to terms with this audience as, for example, *My Beautiful Laundrette* did, would have allowed *Playing Away* a much wider range of connections, and *Handsworth Songs* and *Passion of Remembrance* a much more direct political element.

While all three films break with any notion of essentialist identity in terms of subject mater, they resurrect it at the level of address. Realism presupposes a unified audience procluded at the level of the natural language, modernism presupposes a unified audience in terms of a future as yet not quite realised and which the text itself will bring into being.

The realisation that there are no essential identities needs to be paralleled by the realisation that there is no single audience, that the national culture cannot be understood as a totality which provides a unified audience but as a series of differences, a multitude of audiences. To take such a position is immediately to allow a much more plural set of aesthetic values than has been permissible within the western tradition or, at a more local level, than was evident in the debates about the films we are discussing today. It is from this perspective that we can build on the achievements to which all three films contribute.

Colin MacCabe is Head of Production at the British Film Institute. His many publications on film, literature and popular culture include *Theoretical Essays, High Theory/Low Culture* and *Futures for English* (Manchester University Press). He is editor of *Critical Quarterly* and has contributed to various television programmes including *Big Words, Small World,* for Channel 4.

Two Kinds of Otherness: Black Film and the Avant-Garde

Judith Williamson

I'm going to start from where Stuart Hall finished off. When he was talking about the possibility of a criticism that would neither hold up certain independent films quite uncritically as being 'right on', nor criticise them from a mainstream position – that's really what I've been trying to do over the last few years on the *New Statesman*. And I want to talk, not only about criticism, but about the kinds of forms available for film-makers engaging in oppositional practice, and the way our notions of those forms cross with issues of race to produce a sort of doubly Other cinema. Finally I want to try and resuscitate the question of class, which recently seems to have been dropping right out of the race-gender-class trilogy.

I'm starting from my own position as a critic because part of what I try to do in my work is to engage with mainstream criticism. In practice that means for example that in doing a critique of *Sammy and Rosie Get Laid*, a film I really didn't like, I had to spend about a third of my column engaging with Norman Stone's reactionary attack on it and carrying on that debate with other critics while trying to
criticise the film as well. I think that's the kind of thing Stuart was talking about and it's quite a difficult thing to balance.

But I'd like to make a distinction between mainstream criticism and mainstream cinema. This is really quite important. Whilst I would say I'm totally hostile to mainstream critics and the kinds of assumptions underlying almost all the cinema criticism in the national press today, I don't feel the same extreme opposition to all forms of mainstream cinema. And I think its important *not* to collapse together, as the oppositional movement often has done, a cinematic – ie. film-making – practice and a critical practice. It's become a sort of tenet of the oppositional area of cultural politics we all move in (and not only in film) that practice and criticism go hand in hand, until they're almost seen as the same. This collapsing together – which is part of the whole '70s notion of theoretical – practice-as-part-of-practice thing – has I think to some extent gone past its useful point. Because, as I said it's important to me to be able to attack mainstream critics, but not always to sweep out everything within mainstream cinema at the same time – certainly not to sweep out the mainstream cinema *audience*, which is what I'm referring to when I talk about class in this context.

I'll come back to that point, but for now I'm setting up this slightly unfashionable dichotomy between film making practice and criticism or theory because I want to consider the effects of their elision on the kind of oppositional area that most of us work in. I was educated as a Marxist to understand the relation between theory and practice as a dialectical relationship, where theory isn't a blueprint for action but, almost the reverse, an attempt to find translatable patterns in what *has* happened, translatable in that they can be used to help understand other situations and prevent repeating mistakes. So as I see it, theory isn't so much a set of guidelines for what to do, but a sort of stock-taking where you try to get to grips with a situation. I'm saying this because most of us feel the pinch of

certain orthodoxies that have grown up around what you could very loosely call 'Screen theory', where oppositional cultural theory and people are now working in an area which sometimes feels every bit as rigid as the orthodoxies of the dominant cinematic practice we're meant to be against.

I'm not saying I disagree with oppositional theories, in fact I'm one of the main people who's always going around saying they should be *more* oppositional, but I'm trying to diagnose something about the atmosphere in the field of independent, oppositional film making within which the new work from black film-makers here is broadly located. I do believe our fear of criticism from one another is sometimes stronger than our engagement with those people 'out there' who we don't actually know, but who are, in fact, the readers or viewers of our work. This fear and the anxiety that goes with it have crippling results for film-makers and critics alike. And what happens when people can't make or take criticism openly on a professional level is that it goes underground and becomes far more snide, which in turn fuels people's fear of being criticised, and so on and so on.

This is probably the moment for me to say something which I think has to be said (and hasn't been because there's only one person so far that might have said it) which is that, while I don't feel uncomfortable about it, there are problems with being a white critic speaking in an event like this and writing about black film practice. Without wanting to make too crude an analogy or simply superimpose race and gender, I know I have spent years personally complaining about male critics edging in and intervening within feminist debates about films and I am aware that I could be in a similar position here. I'm saying this not as an apology – since I was invited to speak at this event – but because it isn't often discussed and there seems to be enormous embarassment around this area. I've found – at a pragmatic level of noticing what people say in private and comparing it what they will say or write in public – that there is a reluctance by white critics to make criticisms of films by black film makers because they feel (sometimes quite rightly) not qualified to do so, or to put it more bluntly, they are afraid of appearing racist.

I don't want to spend too much time picking out particular films, but for example I have yet to read or participate in a free-ranging critical discussion of *Passion of Remembrance*. On the one hand I think it's quite right that white critics should hesitate when they are confronted with films coming out of a different experience from their own. But on the other hand, there are, to continue being blunt, problems with being a white critic in a different way because it makes criticisms which may have some substance more easily dismissable. Kobena Mercer has written in a paper on the aesthetics of black independent film in Britain that white critics' and audience's perception of the 'influence of Euro-American avant-garde cinema and film theory' on works like *Passion of Remembrance* and *Handsworth Songs* 'suggests an underlying anxiety to pin down and categorise a practice that upsets and disrupts fixed expectations and normative assumptions about what 'black' films should look like'[1]. I'm raising this particular piece of argument because it pre-empts my main point, which deals precisely with this issue, the place of avant-garde cinema, or rather, of these films within that place. The issue of theory I've already tried to deal with a bit. Anyway, whatever the status of my perceptions are as a white critic I just think the point had to be raised and it would be a strange day if nobody said it so I'm saying it.

Another Other

Coming back to what I would call oppositional criticism, the one loosely based around *Screen* or which operates in the area of developing critical practice that Stuart was outlining – within this sphere there is another kind of good/bad dichotomy alongside the one he described. And I'm glad he was the person that said it: a film made by a black film maker is not 'good' automatically because the director is black any more than a film made by a woman is good because its made by a woman. Basically he's saying goodbye to the simplistic Black-Film-Good/White-Film-Bad dichotomy in favour of a more complex way of understanding the politics of ethnicity. Of course, just saying this doesn't change things overnight and I think it will be some time before those black films which are especially in the limelight at the moment lose their aura of untouchability. Apart from making the critic's job more difficult, that aura must in many ways be a burden to the film makers, who have to be constantly producing show-pieces and be on show themselves, a position which in my experience has never helped anyone to develop their work, and which reflects somewhat dubiously on the film culture that makes such demands. Those demands are, in a sense, a part of that polarity Stuart described and in the long run I think it will be the highly pressurised, young black film-makers who benefit most from his attempt to dismantle this simple equation of black film making with 'Good' film making, an equation which keeps it locked in a particular kind of Otherness.

But besides that Good-Bad orthodoxy centred on race which Stuart described, there is another kind of orthodoxy within this critical arena, another Good/Bad dichotomy which, to parody it rather crudely says, Realist, narrative, mainstream cinema : Bad ; non-narrative, difficult, even boring, oppositional cinema : Good. We must all be familiar with this, and whether or not one agrees with that formulation, it has had a great influence on the kinds of positions people can take up as filmmakers or critics. Pursuing my analogy with Stuart's point: there's another Other that I want to tackle from my position as film critic, which is the avant-garde as the Other of Hollywood cinema.

We've all become adept at handling this term: as women and feminists we have become skilled at understanding our position as 'Other' to male culture, and the whole black political movement has for years put forward very highly developed theories and perceptions of how the black functions as 'Other' to white culture. Within film criticism I'm constantly confronted with the avant-garde or the

'difficult' as the 'Other' of Hollywood or mainstream cinema and I think this otherness is just as problematic a relationship, just as much inscribed within what it's supposed to be different from.

I'm only going to invoke one theorist in this talk but I think the work of the French writer Bourdieu is really useful in theorising the way that the place of the avant-garde in art or film as the oppositional or the difficult is one that's actually written into and circumscribed by the culture to which it's meant to be opposed[2]. I'm not trying to be all gloomy and suggest that one can never do anything different or oppositional or make new forms that will push people's perceptions beyond the usual – far from it; I just think that to be productively oppositional, the place occupied by the avant-garde as the structured – in – opposite of the mainstream is something we have to be aware of.

Of course, the concept of Third Cinema was developed exactly in order to avoid that Mainstream/ Avant-garde dichotomy, in recognition of the fact that neither side of it is inherently oppositional or politicised, or, to put it differently, that the whole polarity can still be completely contained within First-World and colonialist culture. The concept of Third Cinema also presupposes a different constituency, an audience which is neither necessarily the predominantly white mainstream cinema audience nor the (also predominantly white) avant-garde, cinematèque audience. But I don't quite know where that gets us in this context, which, is frankly, closer to the avant-garde than anything else. Looking around the room I see lots of people who were at the Third Cinema conference in Edinburgh where battles were raging about what black Cinema was and whether a straightforward narrative film could be a truly oppositional form of film making. I'm dragging that argument back into *this* conference because the film-makers that Kobena Mercer describes in the article I already mentioned, as drawing on a strong Third World as well as First World inheritance, were actually at that event arguing *against* various African and also black US film makers who advocated what I would call fairly un-avant-garde but politically strident work. The key debate about the possibility or the concept of a black aesthetic or a specifically black form of filmmaking is one that's central here; because if there *isn't* such an aesthetic, then black film makers are faced with precisely the problem which confronts all film makers, in that rather inhibiting context which I set out to describe, – which is how to pitch your work. And related to that, although it's not always within the film makers' control, is dealing with how your work is taken up.

Expeditions Black Audio Film Collective

And that's where my point about the avant-garde comes in. It is particularly striking that the black British work that's been taken up most widely in the world of theory, been most written about and also picked up at festivals, on tours, and so on, is the work that fits most obviously into that category avant-garde. This isn't a criticism of the work and it isn't necessarily the work's 'fault', so to speak. But, again on a level entirely to do with personal observation, the reception in somewhere like New York of Black Audio's and Sankofa's work has as much to do with its being formally inventive and for lack of a better term avant-garde, as to do with its being black, or rather, it's to do with the combination of the two.

What I'm saying is not a criticism but an observation; I think its helpful to make it because the formal properties of those films have somehow, in most of the critical discourse surrounding them, been subsumed into their 'blackness'. Yet, say, a Ceddo film like *The People's Account* is just as 'black'. Coco Fusco has said quite rightly that it's easier to import one's Others than to confront them at home. And I would add – it's sometimes easier to confront the political Other, the Other of ethnicity and, in the case say of *Passion*, sexuality – when it occupies the space of Other in that cinematic dichotomy I was trying to describe. Coco's monograph on the work of Black Audio and Sankofa (who she's arranged a tour for there) is called 'Young, British and Black'[3]. But more accurately, it should be called 'Young, British, Black and Avant-garde', for this is what distinguishes the work she has chosen to tour from that of other equally young, equally British and equally black film makers.

Now I too, like Coco, find the work of these particular groups especially interesting, and that's precisely because I *am* interested in finding new forms and experimenting: with documentary (*Handsworth Songs*) and with narrative (*Passion of Remembrance*). All I'm saying is that we should be clear that black film making and experimental film making are not automatically the same thing. I'm hardly the best person to sound off at a black cinema conference on whether or not there *is* the possibility of a black cinema (though I've always understood that question, in other contexts, as one of audience rather than aesthetics – I'll come back to this). But truly, I don't see how there can be such a thing as a homogenous black aesthetic, as became clear in the disagreements at Edinburgh. Or again, using an analogy with feminist debates – where I feel better qualified to make definite pronouncements – during the '70s those of us involved in feminist discussions about cinema were endlessly having these fights about "is there a women's cinema" (my answer is yes, if it's one that women watch) and 'is there a feminist or female [which I know aren't the same thing] aesthetic' – to which I would be inclined to say 'no'.

I remember a particular debate that took place at the FilmMakers' Co-Op, about whether, if a woman was behind the camera, you would avoid having the voyeuristic gaze, analysed by Laura Mulvey as the male look at the female object[4]. There were actual rows about whether or not it was wrong to have a man behind the camera even if a woman was

directing. Of course it may be a hassle for quite other reasons to have a man behind the camera but I don't think there is anything essential to gender or race about either a gaze or an aesthetic.

There *is* a *cultural* dimension to it, but then that brings us precisely back to cultural forms and how to use them. I've made this detour into feminist territory because when someone asked in the last session 'can a white person make a Third Cinema film' my instinct was to answer 'no'. It's like 'can a man make a feminist film'; my answer to that would be why the hell would a man want to *think* he was making a feminist film. And frankly that response seems to be contradictory having just said there is no inherent female (or black) aesthetic. But there *is* something in between essentialism and a complete denial of people's different positions and experiences, and I think that the more concrete one's analysis of film culture, the more possibilities for it there are.

Difficulty and Class

Looking at the three films at the focus of today's debate (*Handsworth Songs, Playing Away* and *Passion of Remembrance*) you can see very clearly that there are common issues in black politics with which all three are engaging while aesthetically they're all very different. Just from seeing these three films it's obvious that there isn't one black aesthetic. In the light of all this I would say that any kind of oppositional or any questioning cinema is going to have to engage with both mainstream and avant-garde practices, and perhaps challenge that very dichotomy – which after all rests on all those high culture/low culture ideas. Colin MacCabe talked about the outmoded counterposition between realist and avant-garde aesthetics but I'm going into it in more detail because I think you have to find ways to engage with *both* of them. The eliding of these two 'Good/Bad' polarities, with the white film, reactionary, Bad/black film, progressive, Good dichotomy and the mainstream film, realist, Bad/avant-garde film, difficult, Good dichotomy just marrying each other, lets you just fill the avant-gardeness with say a black cinema, so you have a black, avant-garde cinema and it can function as the Other to white mainstream Hollywood stuff. I'm simply trying to draw attention to that other binary structure which I think has already begun to adhere to the first one and to pull apart all those four corners, white, black, avant-garde, mainstream.

This is where I want to come back to audiences because I think audience do matter. I don't see how you can talk about oppositional or political film without talking about audiences. I really don't. I never have done. Audiences *do* matter. It's not enough to say Oh well everythings fractured, everything's just diverse – that's not adequate if your are to be political. If you're political you do want to reach people beyond your buddies; I think lots of issues arise here which aren't specific to black cinema but which are important to it. There are lots of obstacles as well. There's the kind of right-on-ness of the workshop movement, into which the black groups have come fairly late, and it is a problem that the movement as a whole has never successfully grappled with, the question of audiences. Obviously it's a complicated issue and partly it's tied up with funding, money, dependency. The problem that I'm talking about though is that the struggle to set up the workshops, which I myself was involved in, was such a big one that once they were established and funded there was a huge sigh of relief and then people forgot to talk about the products, the actual films.

Thinking about actual films and how they work – I'm glad also that Stuart brought up *My Beautiful Laundrette* because outside the 'Screen' circles that I to some extent move in a lot of people I know who are not at all theoretical just love *My Beautiful Laundrette*. They love it! And many of them are *not*, for example, people who have thought at all about heterosexism. I'm thinking maybe of neighbours, old school friends, not people that I know professionally. It has in some way reached out to people. As Stuart said, it's been a highly *enjoyed* film. In some ways it's an absolutely classic Romance. You're just dying for those people to kiss – and they're both men. And one is black and the other is white. And you're sitting there in the role of the classic Hollywood spectator thinking 'are they going to get off with each other? Is he going to say it? Will he be late?'. The cinematic structures that it employs are completely mainsteam, it is not an avant-garde film in its form at all. There's nothing that interesting about it visually, I don't want to be rude to the makers but it is not a formally exciting work. And yet it had this enthusiastic reception just about everywhere except in what you might call the *Screen* world where it was, well to put it bluntly, kind of sneered at by all those people who are anti-mainstream. I'm afraid I'm drawing on what I actually hear people say but they don't print, and I'm sorry to do that but otherwise these things don't get properly aired. I think these issues are too important to let them slip by in odd remarks – because, as I keep saying, audiences really are important.

So my personal bench-mark of one aspect of political films making would be, that you would want your film – I would want my film – to reach some people, maybe not the whole of the people, maybe not a mass audience, but to reach *some* people who aren't already engaged in the kind of debates we've been talking through, certainly to reach people outside the sometimes esoteric or privileged arena of film theory. This is a very rough and ready definition but it brings the issue of audiences back without saying either this must speak for the whole black community or this must speak for all women, or this must speak for everybody. You simply want your work to reach *somebody* outside your own circles, or at least that's what I want.

In coming back to audiences I think we are coming back to the question of class. I know that what I'm saying might be challenged by the kind of postmodernist analysis that sees everything as already fragmented but when we're talking about mainstream cinema and why people enjoy a film like *Laundrette* we are talking about class, if not in a completely rigid sense, at least in the sense that Bourdieu addresses when he talks about 'cultural capital' – some level of education into film language and forms.

For about the first five or ten years that I ever watched avant-garde films, when I was a teenager, I found it really difficult; it was incredibly hard to learn to expect different things from films, not to expect resolution, not to expect closure, not to expect to care about the characters and so on. *Now*, I can truthfully say that some avant-garde movies are among my absolutely favourite films. But the point is you don't just sit down one day and find 'difficult' films really enjoyable. Without confronting that fact and its connection with class I think we're deceiving ourselves. The reason that I got to be able to like avant-garde films is because I had all that time in college and if you don't want to call it class, call it education or call it cultural capital, to take up Bourdieu's useful term.

We're talking a lot nowadays about race and gender and their relation to representation is being very highly theorised at the moment. But it's interesting that we haven't talked so much about class and representation, because it does raise major formal issues and that is where you come back to notions of difficulty which aren't just to be put aside. I mean the difficulty which is something to do with having a class or educational position different to the one where you learn to sit through *Wavelength* without getting fidgety. Now I can do it but it took me a long time! And these are really things we have to think about.

Having started with my position as a critic I'll end by thinking from the viewpoint of a film maker, because I think a key issue at the moment is the problem of *learning*. It's very out of date at the moment to talk about learning the skills of your medium but nevertheless that's something that filmmakers have to do just as learning to watch rather more difficult films is something that audiences have to do. The whole oppositional movement has a lot to learn about cinematic pleasure. That isn't to say, let's make films in a totally conventional way, but to say, let's reclaim certain kinds of pleasurable cinematic experience without throwing them out with the politically unacceptable bathwater. Any kind of progressive new cinema involves learning how to make films that can engage and be appealing without necessarily running back to precisely the same old realist modes. And part of that learning is actually listening (I know this sounds disgustingly like the Labour Party) to what people say about the films they see.

I'm not holding that up as the only factor in making a film, but I'm emphasising it and I'm finishing on it because I think it's a thing which has been missing in many of these debates. A cavalier attitude to audiences is the very opposite of a politics that's concerned with people changing their perceptions. This may seem to have moved off the subject of black cinema, but perhaps it is a sign of the strength of black film making practice in Britain now that we can stop asking 'what *is* black cinema' and start addressing some of the more complex questions raised by actual films and their audiences, questions which all oppositional film makers could learn from.

Judith Williamson teaches at Middlesex Polytechnic and is the author of *Decoding Advertisements* and *Consuming Passions* (Marion Boyars). She has made one film, *A Sign*

***is a Fine Investment*, and was until recently film
critic on the *New Statesman*.**

Notes

1 Kobena Mercer, 'Diaspora Culture and the Dialogic
   Imagination: The Aesthetics of Black Independent Film in
   Britain' in Mbye Cham and Claire Andrade-Watkins
   (eds.) *BlackFrames: Critical Perspectives on Black
   Independent Cinema*, MIT Press, 1988, p51.

2 Pierre Bourdieu, *Distinction: A Social Critique of the
   Judgement of Taste*, trans Richard Nice, London:
   Routledge and Kegan Paul, 1984.

3 A touring exhibition curated by Coco Fusco and
   produced by Ada Griffin, presented by Third World
   Newsreel, New York, May 1988. Monograph available
   from Third World Newsreel, 335 West 38th St. 5th
   Floor, New York, NY 10018.

4 Laura Mulvey, 'Visual Pleasure and Narrative Cinema',
   Screen Autumn 1975, v 16 n 3, pp, 6 - 18.

The Other is In: Black British Film in the US

Coco Fusco

I am going to speak in very specific terms because
America is too vast for sweeping statements, and my
experiences in England are too limited to begin
generalizing about the situation here. Also I was
asked to discuss the more *concrete* issues I face in
attempting to promote Sankofa and Black Audio's
work outside England. But before I talk about what I
am confronted with in the States, I would like to say
a few things about why and how I became interested
in the workshops.

Questions that are put to me here suggest that
there is a tendency to perceive Black America as a
unified, singular entity. This is probably due to the
largely textual relationship that many people here in
England have to it. Nonetheless, this perception
really doesn't facilitate understanding of the fact that
there are many other people of colour in the
Americas, or of the many different cultures that
incorporate African traditions in the Americas. It
also colludes with the particularly North American
assumption that America is the United States.
Although the critical discourse on Third Cinema in
Britain acknowledges the importance of debates on
film culture that came out of the New Latin
American Cinema movement, there doesn't seem
to be the same level of engagement with current
Latin American film, or the cultural politics and
histories that define and divide blacks and Hispanics
in the US: I find this particularly surprising, given the
shared history of migration to and from the
Caribbean and South America, the shared cultural
dynamics in the development of New World idioms,
religions and aesthetics and of colonial legacies.

My own interest in the Black workshops came out of
my perception of the many continuities with new
Latin American Cinema and, to some extent, its
aesthetics[1]. I have been trying to understand what is
happening in black British film culture as both a
mode of aesthetic inquiry into the concepts of race
and diaspora, and as part of a more extended field of
questioning concerning oppositional media
strategies which might prioritize different issues at
different historical moments. And I would like to
point out that, in contradistinction to assertions
made here, the concept and practice of 'Third
Cinema' was originated by white men. I mention this
only to serve as a warning against essentialising and
dehistoricising the term. Finally, my interest in
collaborating with the black workshops stems from
my belief in the positive effects of cross-cultural
fertilization. The exchanges of ideas and arguments
generated here contribute to clarifying issues
concerning politically engaged media that we all –
black, Hispanic, Asian and white – need to discuss.

I cannot separate the question of critical discourse
and black cinema from the work of creating a base in
the United States for Sankofa and Black Audio's
films. I would not say that the audience for such
work is posited as existing only in the future.
Though we cannot assume that an audience exists
for what has been called 'difficult' work, I believe
that it can and must be made through a number of
different means. What I have found is that while
there will always be support from black American
film institutions, as a matter of principle, we are still
faced with a dearth of critical language on black
independent cinema. That support does not

translate into critical response. In general, film culture in the US is far less integrated with academic reasearch. We suffer from the overwhelming presence of Hollywood, it's hold on the mainstream press through advertising, and the populist and/or promotional rhetoric of journalistic coverage.

For those writing outside the mainstream, publishing venues are scarce and even small magazines that have consistently covered Third World film rarely have people of colour on their staff – although this is beginning to change. The film scholarship that is slowly emerging is largely historical, while the reviewing in the black press is aimed primarily at mainstream media and its flaws, relying too often on arguments around 'positive images'. Academic writing on black film lags far behind the more intellectually challenging work developing in black literary studies[2], and the resistance to 'theory' is much stronger in film-making circles. This is due to the legacies of the 60s which the black independent film sector still lives with: *ie*, a powerfully entrenched tradition of realist documentary filmmaking; the belief that accountability and accessibility are synonymous; and the expectations of funders and of the educational market. These legacies fuel a widespread perception that 'experimental' teachniques and 'avant-garde' cinema are Eurocentric, innately elitist and effectively white. Finally, the success of filmmakers such as Spike Lee and Robert Townsend, while motivating programmers across the country to schedule more black films and encouraging backers to invest, is also interpreted and used as proof of the necessity to commercialise.

The New Multiculturalism?

On the other hand, there is a small but relatively powerful and well-entrenched, largely white, avant-garde independent film sector in New York that has renewed its interest in the so-called 'other'. Not unlike here in Britain, this sector has reached a crisis in its own production and theory. There are a few who haven't had a crisis or who have perhaps resolved it by going to Hollywood. Nonetheless the interest in the 'other' has antecedents in the late 60s, when activist filmmakers drew on strategies and theories from third world nationalist movements, and dates even further back if one takes into account the fine arts, the use of African sculpture in cubism, for example. Appropriation from third world cultures by the first world avant-garde is as old as the concept of an avant-garde.

In the contemporary American context, interest in the cultural production of the 'others' substitutes for political engagement. This applies quite aptly to the recent rise in popularity of Latin American film in the US. But this renewed interest in the 'other' should also be seen in light of current cultural policy. In the name of 'multi-culturalism,' non-profit media centres, programmers, and other venues receiving public funding are being pressured to increase their support for 'minorities'. What is crucial to ask in this respect is how the funding slated for 'multi-cultural', 'intercultural' and/or 'minority' work is spent, and by whom? The greatest danger, it seems to me, is that of perpetuating a longstanding division between first world theory and third world activism in its

latest variant, as well-endowed entities are awarded funds to engage in critical thinking about their institutionalized racism, while smaller, less empowered groups outside the mainstream are compelled to revel in their ethnicity to qualify for the little funding they receive.

This doesn't entirely explain the growing fascination in the US with what is happening in the black British workshops. It is quite unusual for independents at this early stage of their careers to be invited so often to present their work in the US. While the workshops have been slighly mystified by many American independents, this doesn't exactly explain why bastions of media culture that have demonstrated little or no interest in black film over the last fifteen years now want to have black *British* independents at their conferences and festivals. It is important to bear in mind that it is much easier and more expedient to import the 'other' and the other's issues than to face them from within, where there is competition for funding, press and popularity. And films that appear to interface with a Euro-American avant-garde film tradition are particularly inviting.

For the many in the US who lack a specific knowledge of the black British cultural and political context, there is a tendency to interpret Sankofa and Black Audio's work through familiar models. To insist on the workshops' direct descendance from Brecht and Godard becomes a way of implicitly insisting that modernist aesthetics are naturally 'colour-blind', and that theorizing the specifity of race is therefore unnecessary. I am not arguing against making reference to Brecht or modernist aesthetics, but I would caution against allowing it to establish hegemony over critical discourse. Maintaining an ironic distance from dominant, imposed, and/or pre-existent discourses is recognized by many as a key characteristic of cultural manifestations in the black diaspora, and as a sign of resistance to colonial domination. A critical discourse on black British cinema must be of a latitude that can include these different readings, as well as their coincidences.

One of the most significant things for me about Sankofa and Black Audio's films is that in not being monological they address a variety of audiences. The programming plan and publicity strategy I have been working on with Third World Newsreel in New York targets a number of different venues chosen to draw in those different audiences. This means shaping the presentation of the programme to their diverse interests. My interactions with these 'interest groups' (Black American, Afro-Caribbean, gay and lesbian, avant-garde film enthusiasts) – have indicated that no single group could function as the ideal audience. I've encountered anti-intellectualism from some, homophobic hesitancy from others, and a willed ignorance from many who claim that Sankofa and Black Audio are borrowing their aesthetics illegitimately or that they are simply this year's model.

The only way I propose to break down all these problematic assumptions is to work on several fronts through different forms of cultural production, including (but not exclusively) criticism. We must be able to demonstrate that limited visions of black cinema and black identity won't hold. And I feel very strongly that while such endeavours should rely on and develop the strength of black film institutions, it is also important and worthwhile to make the effort outside black communities. Not only do I not support the kind of separatism that not doing so would imply, but practically speaking, film is a cultural form that relies on building many different audiences to sustain it.

Coco Fusco has contributed critical reviews on film culture to *After-Image, Screen* and the *Village Voice*. She has curated touring exhibitions of New Latin American cinema and black British film in the US and currently works as Program Officer for the New York Council for the Humanities.

Notes

1   See, Coco Fusco (ed) *Reviewing Histories: Selections from New Latin American Cinema*, Buffalo NYC, Hallwalls Contemporary Arts Centre, 1987.

2   See, Henry Louis Gates, Jr. (ed) *Black Literature and Literary Theory*, London: Methuen, 1984 and *'Race', Writing and Difference*, Chicago: University of Chicago, 1987.

In Circulation:
Black Films in Britain

June Givanni

Film publicity, marketing and distribution involve a conception of film culture in terms of markets, products and consumers. These terms may not sit well in what is a culturally oriented event such as this conference, but if the development of black British film is to be addressed then they need to be examined in a practical and realistic way. Too often the realities of the marketplace are clouded by generalised rhetoric, which can lead to much wasting of time and resources through inappropriate action and strategies. By looking at issues in the distribution and exhibition of black films in Britain, I want to touch on the question of audiences in a little more practical detail. But I want to start with the economic realities of distribution, as they are crucial.

Financial returns from successful films should yield funds back to the producers and in the case of independent and workshop-based productions, such returns could – theoretically – be used to achieve a greater degree of financial independence for future productions. However, in practice, this is rarely achieved. The levelling-off point for even the most successful film is reached soon after expenses and basic production costs have been met. Thereafter, returns tend to trickle in, slowly – if at all. What distribution does is enable those involved in the production – from the production company, script-writer, director, actors and actresses to technicians – to become known to a potential audience. As audiences become more familiar with independent or workshop-based productions, such films become more commercially viable to the investors, who work with a commercial imperative to maximise returns, and/or satisfy the demands of funding institutions (often state agencies) who are more concerned with the cultural status of the products.

With this in mind, it would be useful to note that when we refer to 'black independent film', this category subsumes a wide range of practitioners and areas of operation. On the one hand, there are the black film workshops – funded for revenue and production costs mainly by Channel 4 television, the British Film Institute, and local authorities. Workshops such as Black Audio Film Collective, Ceddo Film and Video Collective, Macro, Sankofa and Retake are supported in this way. On the other hand, there are independent black film-makers and production companies who receive no revenue funding as such, but who are often commissioned by broadcasting companies like Channel 4 or the BBC, or who occasionally receive production finance for specfic projects from the BFI, the Arts Council and regional Arts Associations. Examples of individuals and companies operating in this fashion are Penumbra Productions, Kuumba Productions and directors like Horace Ove and Lionel Ngakane. There are also black production companies who produce programmes or series exclusively for Channel 4, such as Bandung Productions who produce *Bandung File*, the black and Third World current affairs programme, and Azad Productions who have produced the series *Sunday East*, an Asian magazine programme. And in addition, there are of course many individual black film and media professionals who work in partnership with white colleagues in a number of independent production companies.

The wide range and nature of practices and funding sources suggests that different practitioners seek different types of exhibition for their work – from theatrical release to smaller scale exhibition at regional film theatres, 'art' cinemas and local community venues, or other forms of exhibition such as broadcast television and (another medium which is highly relevant, but not often mentioned) video. Choices about the different forms of exhibition often follow from the sources and amounts of money invested in the production. In this sense, funders and funding have a determining influence on what gets made and where it gets shown. The work that exists so far in black film-making may thus reflect the constraints and expectations of funding bodies as much as the priorities of the film-makers themselves.

At the same time, funding agencies want to see evidence of that elusive black audience; it's an important item on their shopping list. Audiences are who films are made for – or are they? What audiences are black film-makers aiming to reach with their work? And whose pleasures do they hope to provide? The funders'? Their own? Black peoples'? The masses? Most film-makers would argue that their concept of who the films are made for is a mixture of all four. However, a major issue in exhibiting black independent film is how to sensitise cinema and television audiences who have grown up with material that confirms commercial values and traditional expectations. Films such as *My Beautiful Laundrette* and *She's Gotta Have it* have been cited as evidence of wider possibilities for a mass audience for independent films dealing with black themes, issues and perspectives. In marketing jargon, these relatively low-budget feature films have 'crossed-over' from small art-house audiences to achieve commercial success in high street cinemas. But in the case of these two recent productions, this has as much to do with the novelty-value of the plots and characterisation as much as any other aspect of the films. In reality such possibilities for black films cannot be predicted and the potential for 'crossover' is limited.

This is due, in part, to the relatively low production profile of black films in Britain; it is not simply a 'distribution' problem as such. It is unlikely that existing black films will simply cross over, mainly because of the limited range of material produced – limited that is in its format and subject-matter. From a listing of black films made in Britain published by the BFI[1] the following figures – largely comprehensive – give an indication of the spread of work by black UK film-makers currently in distribution. From the section that deals with black films in circulation in the country, there is a total of 130 films and videos. Indicating the nature and type of films made, 67% are documentaries and 33% are fiction. The statistics relating to medium and format are also revealing: 50% of the total number are video productions (rather than 16 or 35mm film) and 86% of the total are under 60 minutes in running time.

To be clear about the problems facing those involved in exhibiting black film, we have to acknowledge the fact that we are not talking about a quantitively substantive body of work, however innovative and challenging it is in qualitative terms. What we are talking about is a varied yet emerging cinema and we should be clear about its limitations if we are to effectively realise its potential and prepare the market for its growth.

If 'bums on seats' are seen as the only marker of success or the only raison d'être for film-making, then the work of black independents in Britain appears unsuccessful in commercial terms. However successful the films are culturally, the fact remains that the paucity of work in distribution creates problems for programmers. Many programmers are constantly searching to bring material in from abroad to supplement the work they are doing in programming black British material. Many have found that *thematic* programming is an effective way of showing black British work, which has been imaginatively programmed alongside material from Third World cinema in many of the seasons and programmes put together by the Vokani exhibition circuit in the Midlands, the Ritzy Cinema in south London or the screenings held by Ceddo and Retake.

Hotel London Retake

This is not to suggest that such practice is merely pragmatic. By featuring work from black America (which includes that of white directors) or from the various traditions in Indian cinema, cultural connections are being made and diverse film forms, styles and languages are being compared[2]. However, programmers in certain parts of the country with few black people see the work as purely 'ethnic-interest related'. Although some regional film theatres have shown black independent work, some more successfully than others, no film societies or large cinema chains have hired black films unless they have been distributed via major companies or receive critical acclaim in the national press. Some cite economic reasons for their hesitant attitude, but the argument that black films are not shown because there is no local black community is shortsighted in the extreme.

The preponderance of films in short and medium-length formats also affects programming decisions. Here arguments about the limited concentration spans of the audience, the cost of using a number of shorts in one programme or audiences' unfamiliarity with shorts with a main feature, all tend to deter programmers from using black independent film. However, small repertory cinemas who do attempt to include more black films on a regular basis sometimes programme a black short with a feature or run double features. Those who approach programming in this way find that it works fairly well with audiences, but it does mean that little or nothing is paid for the short film and that returns on double features are greatly reduced. In these situations such exposure of black film has more to do with building up an audience and developing awareness and taste for such work, rather than recouping elusive profits.

Audiences

The question of audiences underpins all of these issues of programming, exhibition and distribution. Minority audiences relate to concerns with ideas, experiences and cultural values as well as entertainment. Black workshops, for example, tend to want to present their work with the opportunity to discuss it with such target-audiences, as they see feedback as important to their development. In this situation, what is needed is a way of building upon what is now a minority audience by attracting audiences to venues that are consistently trying to programme black film-making. This latter point suggests that there may be a role for a black film venue in the quest for mass appreciation of black cinema.

This is a controversial suggestion, as some believe such a venue would marginalise black films even further and that rather than reach a wider mass audience it would tend to ghettoise black film. But the question remains: how can we consistently build a public profile for black films? How can we encourage a wider audience? Seasons in mainstream venues like the National Film Theatre are important, but because they are intermittent, audiences have to be built anew each time – efforts and resources are thereby often duplicated. Considerations about where and how a black film venue might function must now enter the arena of debate. While such a venture would aim to attract the widest possible audiences, I suspect that another important goal would be to encourage more black people to come out and see black films. Within the framework of such a venture, new styles of programming could be considered, placing film and cinema in relation to other arts – for example, cinema and music is a marriage to be pondered on. Music is often held up as the model for mass 'crossover' success: black music has changed the profiles of many national music and recording industries (although there are still discriminatory practices in this and other cultural industries). The mass appreciation and popularity of black music could be seen as an ideal that many film-makers would like to achieve.

Meanwhile, black film-making should be recognised for its distinctive contributions to what is known as 'British' film culture and there are issues to be explored here about the place of black film-making in a 'national' film culture which is experiencing a crisis, both creatively and economically. What is important for future generations and for up-and-coming black film and video makers is that

the achievements of black film be valued and recognised. Hopefully, in addition to practical changes in the areas of distribution, programming and exhibition, the development of criticism and appreciation will provide a basis on which we can move on and stop re-inventing the wheel.

June Givanni is a freelance consultant on distribution, exhibition and programming of black and Third World film and video. Among the many conferences she has co-ordinated are *Third Cinema* at the 40th Edinburgh International Film Festival and recent film festivals in Boston and Martinique.

Notes

1 *Black and Asian Film and Video List*, compiled by June Givanni and edited by Nicky North and published by Study Materials, British Film Institute, 1988.

2 Pioneering examples of such imaginative programming were the *Third Eye Festival* held at three London venues (Bloomsbury Theatre, Rio Cinema and Ritzy Cinema) in October-November 1983; and the *Anti-Racist Film Programme* held at numerous schools, youth clubs, libraries, churches and community centres between November 1984 and March 1985. Both seasons were produced and presented by departments of the Greater London Council.

Channel 4 and Black Independents

Alan Fountain

What I propose to do is to make a series of remarks which, I hope, will shed some light on the general issues under discussion. It seems to me that the advent of Channel 4 represented the possibility of a source of money to enable black work in the independent sector to develop and also, as importantly, to find another means of exhibition — namely, television — for black work to reach wider audiences. So at the outset one could say that there was a possibility for the flowering of work and for increasing diversity. Although there is really not enough time to go into the complexities of what actually happens at Channel 4, I want to make two points about this stage in the development of black film-making.

One is that it seems to me that the diversity is more potential than actual and that we still await that diversity, or rather what I mean is that we still await the Channel's real interest in that diversity. June Givanni has pointed out a whole number of organisations and individuals who have a place in what can overall be described as a black production sector involving, in one way or another, film-makers who have worked in relation to Channel 4. But I think there is a slight problem in not recognising the diversity of this sector, even within a conference such as this. There is something infinitely pleasurable, interesting and fascinating talking about the two films which have been at the focus of debate — *The Passion of Remembrance* and *Handsworth Songs* — and there is, I think, a general agreement at a meeting of this sort that, whatever we may individually think or whatever criticisms one might want to make, that these films are welcomed, that they are liked, that broadly speaking they are seen as a breakthrough for black film-making.

Now I agree and place myself firmly in that camp; but I also think one can learn as much if not more from some of the problems and difficulties as well as the successes of black independent production if you look at a much wider range of work. It is a pity that we can't debate a greater number of films against a much broader canvas, in order to go into more detail about what black production actually is on the ground. Virtually all those film-makers and workshops and individuals involved would define themselves as constituting a black production sector. It *is* important to recognise that there are other films and other strategies as well as the few we're looking at today.

One point which is related to that and has something to say about the difficulties we face in analysing, assessing and understanding what is happening in the black production sector is that there is considerable pressure inside Channel 4, and for the producers I work with, to deliver successes in the elusive sense of what Channel 4 means by 'success'. What is it that you make to be successful in Channel 4 terms? What 'successes' will guarantee the continuation of my work or the continuation of my department or say the work of Farrukh Dhondy's department and what then will also guarantee the continuation of funds going out to black work?

The point is that the many pressures for success necessarily produce difficulties — tensions, competitiveness, defensiveness — and contribute to a sort of paranoia within each of the sectors that

Channel 4 works with. It is also difficult, when working under day-to-day production pressures, to have a more distant, more principled or more politicised debate about what is it that everyone is engaged in. Of course we would want to say more than that but I feel one has to recognise there is always a problem arising for the film-makers who are trying simultaneously to work in a sector that wants to collectivise and share a broad solidarity when, at the same time, within that sector, there is a fairly high degree of competition.

The next point I would like to raise, is that the black production sector is still in an early phase and that it is relatively early to make final assesments about what has gone on.

That might seem to be the predictable view that someone like me would come up with, but I simply want to emphasise a point raised by June's contribution, which is that there is an enormous sense of disparity between what has actually been produced and what it is we can usefully talk about. Although we recognise the impetus given to black production by Channel 4 and the GLC — the opportunities this opened up such that a lot of younger people were able to find some space for their aspirations — it is important to acknowledge that we are still only talking about a relatively small body of work. I feel very strongly that the most important thing that can happen is for more and more work to be produced so that there is more and more debate about it. Another point I'd relate to this, bearing more conceretly on the issue of opportunities, is that it is not at all obvious to me that we can assume that the relationship black producers and practitioners have with Channel 4 will automatically flow on without interruption. That dosen't seem to me to be self-evident at all. To put it another way: what is it that has been produced so far that would go on?

In the current fluctuating state of film and television there is a whole analysis to be made of the terms under which one can go on producing for a changing organisation like Channel 4. And with the supposedly new opportunities of BBC and ITV commitment to 25% of independent production, it seems to me that there will be an ever-changing problematic around funding, with a lot of fraught negotiation with those companies. Clearly this has important implications for work which is more controversial because of its content.
Judith Williamson was quite right to spot that what the IBA and Channel 4 didn't really like about Ceddo's film *The Peoples Account* was it's political content. Their response to the film gives a fairly clear warning of the problems that lie ahead. There are areas of work that we might like and want to go on seeing, financing and making which are compatible with actually quite nasty regimes in television — and there is another sort of product which media authorities don't like because they see immediately what it represents.

Diversity

Having laid out some general themes I want to move on to some of the films I have been more centrally involved with. I want to stress initially the importance of maintaining a variety of different sorts of work, as we need diversity within the independent production sector generally, let alone the diversity (actual or potential) that other departments within Channel 4 represent. I see two important aspects of that diversity which need to be placed in perspective. The first is, just to reiterate, that I do very much welcome the work of Sankofa and Black Audio, the two workshops behind the productions we have focussed on. What they've done does represent a breakthrough, and there is something very exciting about the work. I also think it is worth saying that you haven't seen anything yet from those groups – they are just beginning. The new projects they are planning, writing scripts for, and so on promise *more diversity*. It is going to take time to develop and reach wider audiences and I think, although the film-makers can speak for themselves, that considerations of audience are very important. I'm sure many of you know that this is something that has been passionately debated within and between the workshops and I think that not all, but some of the future work will take much more specific directions: some perhaps being smaller and more experimental, some moving towards the mainstream as the examples of so-called crossover films have shown. I think over the next couple of years a lot of the worries expressed today will be resolved, although there will probably be a new set of worries to replace them – there always is.

Second, it seems to me that the reasons those particular films are important is that they are central to the current moment; they tackle the whole notion of the nation, of Britishness, of Englishness – a nation which is currently being thrown into crisis. If these concepts have to be completely re-thought, then films like *Passion* and *Handsworth Songs* and the work that these groups are continuing to do have an important and fundamental role to play. Even though there may be problems of audience in relation to these two films specifically, what they are trying to get to grips with is of fundamental political importance.

I would also like to say that as someone personally involved in backing that area of work and backing the cultural politics that Stuart Hall eloquently described, I personally don't want to throw out other forms of work just because they look a bit more conventional. There is a danger of assuming that 'well, there has been a lot of black film-making and the new work makes a lot of that other work redundant', but I personally do not have any intention of not continuing to show an interest in relatively conventional documentary work. I don't think that one replaces the other, and *The People's Account* is an extremely instructive example of the importance of such work. People I'm sure have a whole variety of views about it as a programme but one of the things I think it is important to take on board is that whatever reasons the IBA and Channel 4 come up with for refusing transmission on Ceddo's terms[1], the thing they really didn't like about it – what outraged the crucial people in both organisations – was seeing teenage people saying, 'this isn't going to work anymore, we are going to destabilise the society until you take an interest in what we have got to say'. It was this 'voice' that the authorities didn't like.

Now it seems to me that such a voice does have its own important place in this whole process of re-definition, of re-understanding the notion of the nation, of Britishness and of Englishness and this is the voice which television is extremely afraid of – even of seeing it on the screen let alone actually handing money over to groups who make such programmes. This raises another point which is in danger of being overlooked; the question of how to close the gap between producers of films and their audience. It comes back then to the rather old notion of trying actually to involve people who are normally thought to be the audience in the process of production itself, that is in making their own images. This means breaking the gap that Stuart Hall discussed, where certain groups are always the object of the camera, where it's always someone else turning up at Broadwater Farm[2], someone else who has got the money and got the camera and who's saying what they want to say about you. It is really important for me to go on arguing that there should and must be a space in television for this sort of work and that there is money to go to where some producers want to engage in that difficult, demanding and often very unrewarding type of work with groups of people in the community. Often it is not very interesting aesthetically, but it is important. Also I am not suggesting that there is one community or that we can somehow represent it all in one film, but the importance of this sort of work is that it takes a particular group, a particular association or a particular political perspective and works to put something on the screen that they want to see on the screen. That to me is an important part of what I see as a valuable diversity of programme making. It may be based on notions of access, of community, of accountability – all of which might be problematic – but I think there is a danger of letting all that go.

I would just add a couple of points about audiences in this context. The one fairly broad issue about audiences, which I have discussed with June Givanni over many years, is how to get more money into the programming and exhibition of black work and how to get circuits of distribution and exhibition to work much more efficiently for black and Third World films. Now, what I say may sound defensive, but I think that Channel 4 does represent an advance in the sense that even in the horrible ghettoised monster represented by the Eleventh Hour[3], you do get beyond an audience that already knows about the films. Undoubtely most Eleventh Hour programmes do that. This might not meet Judith Willamson's criteria for a popular film and I'm not trying to make a personal advertisement either; what I am trying to do is to argue for taking television seriously. The point about television as a medium for exhibition is that every time you reach an audience of more than 300,000 and once you get half a million and then once you get a million or a million and a half, you are hitting a lot of people who almost certainly won't before have come across what you are saying to them. To my mind, the struggling relationship to television isn't just about finding sources of money, it's about reaching people all over the country. I think sometimes the whole independent sector forgets that, and instead Channel 4 is used like any other funding agency –

which in my view is a politically irresponsible position to take in relation to television.

There is also the whole question of change which we are faced with at Channel 4 now, not just because Jeremy Isaacs has gone, but because the Channel has entered a second phase and people are asking: what is going to happen from now on? Basically, I don't think that this is the time to relax if one is going to take television seriously.

My final point comes back to the workshop sector, because what the black workshops have shown is that working in that way, they have made fantastically productive use of a particular space, at a particular time, which is completely different from the usual commissioning process at Channel 4. I know there is a great deal of debate about whether workshop production processes really are that different – and I think the answer is that they are – but the essential point is that it would have been very difficult for black film-makers and producers to make the sort of work the workshops have produced if it was done through a straightforward commissioning process. This is because the pressures of time and money are too intense and what they force people to do – regardless of their will – is to 'go conventional', because that is what you can do quickly. If you have to deliver a documentary in two weeks, unless you are very talented and very skilled and have been doing it for years, then you probably go back to something that is pretty basic and routine. What I think the workshops have achieved is to get a little more time and a little more space to play around a little bit and therefore make important breakthroughs. My basic message is 'forward to the next phase' – and I feel very optimistic about it.

Alan Fountain is Commissioning Editor for Independent Film at Channel 4. Since its inception, he has played a key role in interpreting the Channel's commitment to diversity and innovation.

Notes

1 Ceddo's experiences with the IBA over *The People's Account* are documented in articles reprinted in the film-makers' dossier.

2 The Broadwater Farm Estate in Tottenham was the scene of 'riots' in 1985, provoked by the death of local resident Mrs Cynthia Jarrett. The events took place within weeks of disturbances between police and black communities in the Handsworth area of Birmingham. The reasons for both are discussed by Stuart Hall and A Sivanandan in *New Socialist*, n32, November 1985.

3 The *Eleventh Hour* is Channel 4's independent film and video showcase, transmitted late night on Mondays.

Nothing But Sweat inside my Hand: Diaspora Aesthetics and Black Arts in Britain

Paul Gilroy

I want to raise some questions about how we can begin to look at the film-making which is being discussed and celebrated here in a broader context – the context of what might be called 'The Black Arts Movement' in this country. I want to touch on some of the politically important questions which June Givanni and Alan Fountain have already raised; but there is more to be said about aesthetic questions as well.

I want to suggest that what's in order is an agenda of problems, not just for film-makers but for the black arts movement as a whole. The most productive way to proceed is to think about how certain antagonisms might be sharpened, with a view to giving this 'community' a way of having disagreements publicly and productively, rather than simply rationalising the domination which exists or mystifying the political conflicts which have been touched on here in terms of competitiveness and the market: for example problems of what might loosely be called Emperor's New Clothes-ism that is, the attempt to package and market blackness by creating a spurious air of innovation around it. The best way to do that seems to me to focus initially on the question of representation itself, and in particular on the tension between representation as depiction and representation as delegation or substitution. This can provide a handle for opening up the question of the black film-maker or the black artist in the public sphere as figures in *public* politics. This means coming back to the question which June Givanni raised towards the end of what she was saying. She asked who are these films made for and answered: 'well, there's the funders, there's the artists themselves, there's black people'. I want to push that line of questioning further and ask, 'well, which black people?' – because I don't think we can allow ourselves even that degree of generalisation any longer. I think we have to begin to unpack that apparent unity and look at the different publics, the different audiences which comprise a hierarchy, not just between black and white, but within black communities as well.

The first question for black film-makers then becomes how, or rather whether, they want to deal with the problem of admitting to white audiences as well as black ones. I think it is important to remember that this question assumes different proportions in relation to vernacular cultural forms from those it takes in the more rarified atmosphere of black film-making practice. One way of highlighting that difference is to ask 'really, how different is the black audience for the films we've seen here from the white audience?' Is there for example a black working-class or even a non-working-class audience eagerly anticipating these particular cultural products? Getting a clearer picture of these important issues, and the questions of class and power which they entail, seems to me to be actively hindered by the orthodoxies of racial politics at this time. Fashionable beliefs endorse the idea that racial identities are somehow primary; yet the importance attached to these identities seems to be born out of a fear of their increasing fragility. In places where such things are discussed, it is often deemed such a difficult matter to raise questions of racial identity that black and white people are unable to sit down and talk about it in the same room without their respective identities being thrown into crisis.

Meanwhile, of course, the kind of urban pluralism which is going on outside gatherings like these provides a backdrop of complex syncretism – rather than simple integration – against which the antics of aspiring film-makers are being acted out. Yet even as those kaleidoscopic formulations of cultural syncretism grow more detailed and more beautiful, contemporary anti-racism is perversely entrenching a sense of ethnic difference as something absolute – a break in history and humanity. This new orthodoxy applies, not just to relations between black and white, but *within* the black communities. In particular, it has had a grave impact on the fragile political alliances created between those of African and Asian descent. The notion of a discontinuity between the experiences of these groups has become an article of aesthetic and political faith. This politically disastrous view expresses a mystical commitment to 'cultural insiderism'. It indicates that a mythic longing for cultural homogenisation is alive, not just among the nationalists and the racists who are celebrating Great Britain, but among the blacks and anti-racists as well.

The point I want to pick up from what Alan said earlier is that these rather morbid views of ethnic culture actually get incorporated into the structures of the cultural industries in terms of funding, commissioning and so on. The popularity of these opinions has also bred a rather dangerous political timidity that culminates in a reluctance actually to debate some subjects because they are too sensitive to be aired, too volatile to be discussed openly. Underneath them, like one of those big waves that carries along the surfer, there is a tide of anti-intellectualism. There are some people in the black community who have been eager to accept the trap which racism has set for us, and have begun to celebrate the idea of themselves as people who feel but don't really *think* very much about anything.

Postmodernism/populist modernism

I think that this very peculiar situation actually demands that we return to some old questions, some old, old questions: questions of the autonomy of art, of racial propaganda – the question of whether the couplet between protest and affirmation is an adequate framework for understanding black cultural politics as a whole. In what sense are our artists loyal only to themselves? Can black consciousness and artistic fredom be complementary rather than mutually exclusive? Can there be a revolutionary core to what Richard Wright once called the 'aesthetics of personalism', or to any of the other characteristics of Western modernism in its high form? Nowadays these old questions tend to appear in a somewhat different form and with a different conceptual vocabulary: does something called postmodernism provides a ready-made de-centering of imperial and patriarchal discourses?

I want to suggest that a preliminary resolution of some of these issues is being developed in the practice of a range of different black cultural activists. What I'm proposing may not be a very elegant term, but it is the best one I can think of at the moment; it has an intermediate, heuristic value. There is a resolution of some of these difficulties in what might be called *populist modernism*. This apparently contradictory term suggests that our artists are not just defenders and critics of modernism but that they are at the same time aware of what I regard as their historic responsibility to act as the gravediggers of modernity. This implies a political approach which starts from a recognition of the position occupied by blacks in the diaspora as peculiar kinds of stepchildren of the West – a position which is not confined to the experience of those of us that are of African or Caribbean descent. It is something which is there in the experience of diaspora itself and which ties our various histories of imperialism and colonialism to each other, whether we like it or not.

A populist modernism would also be something which exploited instructively and deliberately that quality of perception which DuBois and other people have called 'double consciousness'. It seems to me that something like that is at work in some of the films shown in the ICA programme. Now, whether that double consciousness, that position *in* but not yet *of* the modern world, is viewed as an effect of oppression or as a unique moral burden, it seems to me to be premised on some sense of black cultures as counter-cultures of modernity – modernity being defined as the period and the region in which capitalism, industrialism and democracy came together so fatefully.

The most basic formal expression of this development can be recognised in the need to articulate a positive core of aesthetic modernism in resolutely vernacular formats. This is something which is not confined to cinema alone, although it marks some of the films that we have looked at. It is shared by a wide range of different cultural expressions. Toni Morrison's *Beloved* for example, seems to me to be doing something of that type. Lenny Henry's recent performances in the character of Delbert Wilkins – in the most recent series of *The Lenny Henry Show* – seem to be doing something similar as well. Now, the term populist modernism shouldn't just be used as a way of marking out these adventuresome black borrowings from and adaptations of a preformed Western canon. It can also be applied where black artists and thinkers have attempted to construct their own distinct sense of modernism that reflects their peculiar relationship to modernity. We have had very intense and particular experiences of the modern world, experiences which evade capture by concepts like 'communicative ethics' and require a special gloss on terms like justice and reason. We also need to emphasise that blacks have their own traditions of inquiry into the politics of representation. These need to be reactivated, resuscitated and drawn on, explicitly rather than implicitly. In particular, they need to be recovered and brought into debates which are just beginning in British cultural politics.

Certain aspects of the aesthetic and philosophical traditions of the African diaspora are particularly pertinent to black Britain's conditions of exile, voluntary and involuntary. They are relevant, firstly, to our understanding of memory not just as a cognitive problem, but as a problem to be addressed in affective and normative terms. Secondly those traditions are pertinent to considerations of the distinctive intertextual patterns in which different texts and performances echo one another, draw on each other, correspond, interact, reply. Thirdly, they demand an explicit concern with the forms of meta-communication which are a property of our own histories. These originate in a historical experience in which, as Charles Davies has pointed out, the error of mistaking a sign for its referent has been very often a matter of life and death[1]. Finally, there is the problem of genre. The constant subversive desire to escape genre is perhaps most evident in some of the literary forms of the black arts movement. The problem of genre is there in the desire to transcend key western categories: narrative, documentary, history and literature, ethics and politics.

Now, approaching contemporary black cultural politics by this route involves a sharp move away from that rigid nexus of modernism/postmodernism and the casual references to the technical successes of modernist culture which sometimes emanate from the orthodoxies of postmodernism. I suppose another way of raising that question is by asking a simpler one: I mean *who* is it that people like Fredric Jameson are talking about when they say 'Our grand narratives are collapsing'[2]. Some of us, who have been denied access to some of the diachronic payoff that people like Jameson take for granted, are just beginning to formulate our own big narratives, precisely as naratives of redemption and emancipation. I want to suggest that our cultural politics is actually not about depthlessness but about depth, not about the waning of affect but about its preservation and reproduction, not about the suppression of temporal patterns but about history itself. What I'm proposing, in other words, is that we shift the centre of debates on the modern experience away from Europe, and look at it from a more supposedly 'marginal' perspective.

The trouble about trying to do this is that here again we bump into the orthodoxies of contemporary racial politics and the way that they have been institutionalised in the funding, commissioning, and reception of films. It is at this point that we need to return to the question of culture – in particular to the issue of ethnic culture, racial culture, as what we need to challenge is the way in which culture is seen as a fixed and final property of social life rather than a dynamic and volatile force. I suppose that the good news is that in spite of the way that some of the more unwholesome ideas of ethnic absolutism have been incorporated into the structures and practices of the culture industry: in the politics of the funding of black arts in particular – the tokenism, the patronage, the nepotism and the competitiveness, that are becoming intrinsic to the commercial policing of black culture – there are still elements within the emerging post-nationalist black arts movement which are prepared to move as black thinkers have moved in the past, towards a global, populist, modernist perspective. I think some of the films we have been discussing are actually moving, uneasily, tentatively, towards that. This is cause for

celebration. It seems to me that in some of those films there is a hesitant, necessary suggestion that black art might begin from the documentation of constructed differences within the fundamental category of blackness. The problem is that, if this is where their movement is to begin, then where is it to end? In the black artist's search for 'space and status'? In the transcendence of racial particularity? In some form of political action?

I want to end by addressing another central problem – which is that the critical tools which are able to unlock and discipline this new movement are at present in a rather undeveloped, foetal state. We can say that this nascent black arts movement's inspiration lies in a more pluralistic understanding, a more polyphonic exploration of the idea of blackness. But how is blackness itself to be understood? Is it a primary identity or a metaphysical condition, or a bit of both? Is Ellison right when he suggests that it is a state of the soul acccesible to all? Was Baldwin correct when he articulated it as a mark of pain and hardship, which carried with it a special obligation to humanise the dry bones of this modern landscape[3]? Perhaps the realisation that blackness is a multi-accentual sign means that we can get out of 'either-or-ism', and that various groups can strive constructively to invest their different black identities in the symbols and forms of our vernacular, expressive culture. Even film culture can provide a means for us to negotiate each other's definitions of race and identity.

Obviously this is a much more complex problem than I have been able to show in this brief presentation. I suppose at the end of the day I want to say that some of us were born here, some of us are struggling to come to terms with our ambiguous, incomplete and subordinate experience of Englishness – at the same time as we connect ourselves to black histories elsewhere and yet also recognise the emptiness of national identities as such. None of us has a monopoly on black authenticity.

Paul Gilroy is Teaching Fellow in Sociology at the Polytechnic of the South Bank, London. In addition to *There Ain't No Black in The Union Jack* (Hutchinson, 1988) he has written widely on black cultural politics and contributed to, *The Empire Strikes Back*, Centre for Contemporary Cultural Studies (1982). He is an editor of the independent journal, *Emergency*, and an occasional DJ and musician.

Notes

1 Charles Davis, *Black is the Color of the Cosmos*, Garland Press, NY 1982.

2 Fredric Jameson, 'Postmodernism, or the Cultural Logic of Late Capitalism', *New Left Review* n 146, July/August 1984.

3 See, Ralph Ellison, *Shadow and Act*, Random House, NY 1964; James Baldwin, *The Price of the Ticket*, Michael Joseph, 1985; and Richard Wright, *White Man Listen*, Doubleday, NY 1957.

'Black Independent Film': Britain and America

James A Snead

From the other side of the Atlantic, it often seems that – especially with regard to funding, distribution, and critical reception – British black film-makers graze in greener pastures than their American counterparts. Americans had their most recent chance to see the latest crop of Afro-British films through the programme on Black Independent Cinema: Britain and America at University of California at Los Angeles (UCLA) in Spring, 1987, and later at 'Blacklight: Chicago's Festival of Black International Cinema in Summer, 1987. Horace Ové, Jim Pines, Maureen Blackwood and others appeared in person to explain their films. These film presentations highlighted differences of theme between Britain and America to be sure, but perhaps more clearly, differences in terms of financing, production, and distribution for alternative film-makers.

The existence of 'establishment' channels for funding and exhibition such as the BFI and Channel 4, as well as the output of various film-making collectives (such as Retake Film and Video Collective, or the Black Audio Film Collective) suggests a vibrant and growing film culture well capable of sustaining the amazing output of 1986, which brought us such works as *Playing Away*, *The Passion of Remembrance*, and *Handsworth Songs*. Moreover, Salman Rushdie's article on *Handsworth Songs* in *The Guardian* – and the ensuing debate – seems from the American vantage point an extraordinary testimony to the importance attached to alternative black films even in 'establishment' circles.

The advertisement for the UCLA program described it as 'a rare opportunity for an American audience to discover the wealth of vital and innovative work being done by black British film-makers, and to gain insight into the political and cultural struggles and achievements taking place in the UK'. Yet it must be said that for most black Americans, seeing black American independent films, or indeed *any* 'independent' films, is a rare opportunity. Despite what seems a relatively greater level of public access in Britain, the major issue on both sides of the Atlantic seems to be, finally, *money* – the lack thereof – both for production-funding and distribution. Better-funded productions – films with high, 'slick' production values – get wider distribution, having the right 'look', and in their turn tend to make enough money to produce offspring, successors, imitators – in short, to create audience demand, and a tradition of films about issues of interest to black people. So questions of political power and ideological control arise as soon as one begins discussing 'black independent film'.

But before I begin to contrast American and British alternative films, I should like to voice at the outset my objections to the unrigorous use of the term 'black independent film' (even though it is a term I am forced to use myself). It is, like the term 'Third World', a conglomeration of compromises which, by the time it is bundled up into a neat phrase, loses most of its intended meaning and often comes across merely as a condescending euphemism for what is really going on. The term seems custom-made to cover-up the 'questions of political power and

ideological control' I just mentioned. It invents some people who just happen to be black and who just happen to have declared some putative artistic and/or financial independence. But artists who have had the term 'black independent' applied to them know how little truth there is in that version of things. It seems to me that this conference has so far been engaged in both a conscious and an unconscious interrogation of the term 'black independent' itself. I want in what follows to continue that discussion.

'Black'

In the first place, what is 'black'? I was at a programme on 'black independent woman film makers' at New York's Whitney Museum in 1986 when a well-known East Indian film-maker stood up and proclaimed that she, too, was 'black', and that her work should therefore also have been given recognition. She caused an immediate uproar among many of the film-makers. There has been a certain over-mystification and over-specification of 'blackness' that has reached the point where some critics and even film-makers suggest that a 'black aesthetic' makes films by blacks as visually distinctive as say, traditional black music is from white classical music. I doubt whether such an aesthetic exists – but even if it did, the resulting taxonomy, while perhaps useful for film critics and historians, would do little to address the vexing ideological and political issues that anyone confronts who is 'non-white'.

Our current 'essentialist' definitions of 'blackness' share the shortcomings of the essentialist ideology of 'whiteness' that has underpinned the course of post-Enlightenment Western history. As a negation of 'whiteness', the terms 'black' or 'non-white', for better or worse, share in this insistent essentialism. 'Whiteness' and 'blackness' lie perpetually at the intersection of *power* and *metaphor*. Certainly skin colour is historical, being a collective sign of the outcome of certain economic and material oppressions and power struggles – processes whose results are still very much with us. Yet colour equally invokes (particularly in a visual medium such as film) certain *metaphorical* chains (white/black, light/darkness, sun/soil, good/evil, purity/pollution, feeling/thought, and so on). These chains of association have most often been used by whites against non-whites, and I believe that no effective political alignment can presume to ignore them. It is as useless to rely upon purely ethnic, anthropological, or sociological definitions (as Stuart Hall's statement seems to suggest) as it is to insist upon an essentialist definition of skin colour. White power has triumphed, after all, as a historical, economic, and finally a *conceptual* form of oppression and hence must be combatted on all these levels of its operation – and more.

Yet the shortcomings of the narrow definition of the term 'black' are everywhere obvious. The fixation upon racial or even ethnic pedigree has tended to separate American blacks from British blacks, American blacks from West Indian blacks, American blacks from Chinese, and Japanese-Americans, American blacks from Hispanic and Latino-Americans, not to mention American blacks from British Indians and Asians. In America, the chief

The People's Account Ceddo

terminological question remains: does 'black' cover Latinos, Asians, Native Americans, and others, or does it just refer to a particular people rooted in the specificity of a particular problematic of slavery, ante-bellum and post-bellum economic and sexual exploitation, and the 20th century's characteristic cycles of protest, repression, and assimilation? The question of 'immigration' and being 'first-' or 'second-generation' British is not immediately intelligible to black American audiences, since indeed for most of us the problem is not the brevity of our sojourn in America, but its unrelenting and unrelieved length.

In Britain, I would imagine that blacks and Asians share similar problems in relation to immigration, racism and assimilation and are more likely to be talking about the same kinds of confrontations with English society – though here, too, there will be important divergences. *Handsworth Songs*, for all its virtues, lacks a theory of non-white solidarity or interaction. *The Passion of Remembrance*, for all its self-reflexivity, does not directly deal with the ethnic differences *within* the black British community: we never learn what are the affinities and tensions between British-Caribbeans and British-Africans, for instance. A broad-based, even militant, usage of the term 'black' as a unifying metaphor is a fitting counter to the pervasive use of 'white' – from Lebanon to Lapland – an an object of cultural identification and ideological bonding. Yet certainly there is also much to be said for preserving the specificity of a historical experience. Indeed, honest film-making requires no less.

Stephen Frears' *My Beautiful Laundrette* written by Hanif Kureishi, for all of its critical success among a small white American audience, was entirely ignored by most of the black press in the US (with the exception of David Nicholson's *Black Film Review* in Washington, DC), because it was, incorrectly, I

think, perceived as being irrelevant to the black American experience. Not incidentally, it is simply a fact that all classes and colours in the US tend to associate any accent that sounds vaguely 'English' (this includes Irish, Australians, and all classes and varieties of British accents) with a vague signified of 'privilege' and 'superiority'. Therefore, it seems both incongruous and even a bit off-putting for blacks to see other black people on screen speaking in British accents, of whatever variety or stripe! Probably the most important window on black Britain for American blacks has been musical, rather than filmic (or both, in the example of music videos of black British rock groups, which are shown quite frequently on the black-owned cable station Black Entertainment Television) with British reggae, and soul groups, such as Club Nouveau, opening up a black British world of which many black Americans were simply unaware.

But ultimately, a narrow usage of the term 'black' is divisive where what is now needed is the forging of new alliances and audiences, and, as I have said, a more vigourous examination of the entire question of an oppressive polity. The fact is, by the term 'black', we are speaking of white privilege and the lack thereof amongst 'others'. What we might usefully begin discussing instead is the existence of *insurgent* or *alternative* cinemas, without mystifying the colour of their producers. Such cinemas would be open to an entire host of adversarial groups and concerns, and, as is beginning to happen in America, would articulate feminist and gay issues, as well as the experiences of various non-white film-makers.

Independent

Secondly, we must ask: what is really meant by 'independent film'? Anyone who has made even the simplest super-8 film knows that that phrase is a contradiction in terms. No film maker is independent in the way that, say, a poet is. Film making, both capital- and labour-intensive, is the *most* dependent art form. This is both a blessing and a curse. So the question has never been one of 'dependence' or 'independence', but merely the nature of one's dependence. At least in the US, film making, more than other art forms, operates under Keynesian, or demand side, economic constraints. Rather than a film being able to seek and find an audience once made, many films without well-defined markets may simply not get funding in the first place. Once more, then, we are dealing with a question of *reception*, but in this case, reception can even pre-empt or censor the actual production of alternative cinemas. (Hence, you cannot *easily* see films by black film-makers in America, British or American, dependent or independent). The questions remain, then: what kinds of statements and images will a society tolerate, where will it tolerate them, and with what frequency?

At best, non-white films, by a kind of Marcusian 'repressive tolerance', become safe totems, tabooed because they ventilate so many of society's own taboos. They say the embarrassing, the unsayable. To some extent, of course, any truthful and articulate black person – whether politician, writer, dancer, actor, or film-maker – is bound to upset the status quo, because, at least in America, his or her very *presence* is an implicit taboo or embarrassment, reminding anyone who chooses to be reminded of America's prior and enduring oppression and exploitation of blacks. All too often, independent films are packed away for discrete presentation in elite museums, late-night educational television programmes, and infrequent, often poorly-attended conferences on 'independent cinema'.

Interestingly, the independent film community itself also encourages a kind of subtle racism: it is generally assumed that if a white film maker's film is 'independent' (ie, underfunded or underproduced), then it may be characterized by some alleged violation of classic realist style, a trait that is judged, depending on the critic, 'experimentalist', 'Godardian', 'amateurish'. Yet the almost universal assumption that high production values are a precondition for 'good' film making tends to work against blacks more forcefully than against whites. A white film may be coded 'independent' and rated critically often on the sole basis of technique, regardless of content. Sloppy film making can be read as auteurist brilliance. Yet if a black film maker's film is 'independent', it is often seen to have been a result of the film's 'content': technical issues are overlooked, even where, as is often the case, they are an intrinsic part of the film's message. Black film makers are seen as furnishing, at best, documentary or raw sociological data. It is considered that the film is good *despite* its technique, not *because of* what I call 'visual recodings' of old stereotyped images of black skin on screen. Even the most successful independent black independent films (such as Spike Lee's *She's Gotta Have It*) have fallen victim to this critical blindness. The reception of these films has usually split along the form/content dichotomy, with their considerable formal innovations being – as in much early criticism of black novels and poetry – sold short for easy sociological discussions of content.

The Difference

Finally, black American and British film-makers seem to be asking different questions about the whole issue of *assimilation*. For black American film makers, the question is not so much 'what would it mean to assimilate?' or 'what is my relation to American-ness'? These questions were settled, mainly in the negative, long ago. To some extent, many black American independent films are preoccupied with the question 'how can I best *keep from* becoming like white Americans? How can I fulfill my personal aspirations and yet preserve my distinctness, my "grooviness" in the stultifyingly squareness of the American context?' For black American film makers, an 'American' identity as such no longer has anything to offer, if it ever did: indeed, the entire history of blacks in America has been the history of whites *taking from*, rather than *giving to* blacks in America (culturally, economically, spiritually).

If we were to invent an 'average' black independent film on either side of the Atlantic, we would find that in America, racism and racial politics, at least in terms of mainstream film imagery, are very much caught up in different conceptual structures from Britain. The North American black remains a former slave who has has moved (not emigrated) to an urban setting from a predominantly rural setting. Both terrains are present in the same continental land mass and are effectively available for film-makers to exploit as their fictional stage. For specific, historical reasons, the roles of 'mammy' (the urban or Southern domestic maid), Uncle Tom (the 'house nigger', household retainer, and quiet collaborator), the black buck (the 'bad nigger', unregenerate, sexy, violent), as well as the agrarian or rural peasant worker, still hover over almost every mass cultural depiction of blacks like unquiet ghosts, and even inhabit the works of black film makers who are trying their best to undermine them. Such paradigms do not play a role in the black British films I have seen.

Furthermore, black American film makers, for all their savvy about street ways and city life, still represent the urban landscape as if it were a hostile territory, as indeed it often is. This tendency, coupled with a recurrent nostalgia for 'Africa', however defined, tends to project an 'other place', a place of deliverance or redemption which is always the potential opposite or counterpart of the urban conditions represented in the films.

In America, 'black independent films' (for want of a better term) fit into three broad groups: what I call 'blacks framed in their place' – films that depict the racist past, or its legacy in the present (paradigmatic limitation); films that show blacks fighting, with only measured success, the white assumptions of black inferiority that code them into place, and that would freeze the status quo; and finally, films that try to achieve what I call 'recoding' through the use of the film medium itself (syntagmatic freedom). It is these latter, formally 'experimental' films, whose technique is largely dismissed as 'sloppy', or 'low budget' film-making.

Finally it seems to me that in black British films, the analysis of the 'structural' crisis of late capitalism in the west is more rigorous, perhaps because these conditions are closer, more concentrated here, and perhaps also because of Britain's more developed tradition of social criticism and political analysis in alternative film culture.

Incitements

I look forward to the day when such questions as we have taken up here may find resonance in diverse settings of reception. In order to nurture the fledgling black cinema movements on both sides of the Atlantic, demand must be stimulated, audiences consolidated, the channels of reception widened. Specifically, mainstream newspapers, such as *The Guardian*, and, to an extent *The New York Times*, must continue to discern in the new black cinema a significant new direction in the history of film, and encourage wider debates on the challenging voices that emerge from these works. Visual media will need increased mass-cultural outlets for films with unconventional themes and opinions. Overall, we need to rethink the 'star' system which has been based on narrow narcissistic identifications for white audiences, a system that tends to discount in advance films with largely unknown black actors (even *She's Gotta Have It* had to be sold as 'Spike Lee's film', with Lee marketed as 'the black Woody Allen' in order to furnish the 'hook' or introductory appeal of the film). Finally, we must remedy the monopoly in black cinema studies of a few books, mostly written over a decade ago: Edward Mapp's *Blacks in American Films*; Donald Bogle's *Toms, Coons, Mulattoes, Mammies and Bucks*; Daniel Leab's *From Sambo to Superspade*; James P Murray's *To Find an Image*; Gary Null's *Black Hollywood* and Thomas Cripps' *Slow Fade to Black* and *Black Film as Genre*[1]. There is not yet a thorough 'history' of British and/or American black independent film-makers, and even these books, for all their merits, have largely misunderstood the developments of the 70s and totally missed those of the 80s. Without getting caught in the trap of applying elistist terminology to presumably anti-elitist works for non-academic audiences, we must promote critically sophisticated chronicles of the extraordinary ferment in black cinematic expression that – against formidable economic and political odds – the last decade has raised.

James A Snead is Associate Professor of English and Film Studies at the Univeristy of Pittsburgh. He has contributed to Henry Louis Gates' *Black Literature and Literary Theory* (Methuen, 1984) and his book, *The Color Black: Hollywood's Uses of Blackness, 1915–1985,* will be published by Routledge in Spring, 1989.

Notes

1 Edward Mapp, *Blacks in American Films: today and yesterday*, City Metuchen, Scarecrow Press, 1972.
Donald Bogle, *Toms, Coons, Mulatoes, Mammies and Bucks: An interpretive History of Blacks in American Films*, New York, Viking, 1973.
Daniel Leab, *From Sambo to Superspade: The black experience in motion pictures*, Boston, Houghton Mifflin, 1975.
James P Murray, *To Find an Image: Blacks in films from Uncle Tom to Superfly*, Indianapolis, Bobbs Merrow, 1973.
Gary Null, *Black Hollywood*, Secaucus, Citadel Press, 1975.
Thomas Cripss, *Slow Fade to Black*, New York, Oxford University Press, 1977 and *Black Film as Genre*, Bloomington, Indiana University Press, 1978.

*Film-maker's Dossier:
Selected Interviews
and Statements*

Going to meet the Man

**Horace Ové in conversation with
Sylvia Paskin.**

HO For me, a director is a director no matter what colour he is. Here in England there is a danger, if you are black, that all you are allowed to make is films about black people and their problems. White film-makers, on the other hand, have a right to make films about whatever they like. People miss out by not asking us or allowing us to do this. We know you, we have to study you in order to survive. In America, they don't have these hang-ups. I know many black directors there who make 'white' programmes. The audience sees a name when the credits roll but not a colour.

When things happen here, like Broadwater Farm or the Brixton riots, I get very annoyed with the media coverage. It is so superficial. They don't do proper research. That is why I made *Pressure*. I was tired of reading in the papers about young blacks hanging around on street corners, mugging old ladies. Nobody tried to find out why they were doing it. The same with *Hole in Babylon* (about the hold-up of the Spaghetti House restaurant by three young blacks and the resulting siege). The men in the siege were represented as a bunch of hooligans. Nobody looked at their background. They never went into the fact that they had a political motivation – that they wanted to set up a centre. One of them was a medical student, one was a poet and writer, and one of them had a background of mental illness.

Pressure Horace Ové

Things may have got a little better since I came here in 1960, when the landladies' signs read, no blacks, no dogs, no Irish. A generation has grown up since then which shares a language and a culture, particularly music. But the racism is still there and prevents black people getting a piece of the action. I think black kids today have got to be prepared to go

beyond these shores and leave England. There is a big world out there waiting, particularly the Third World. You can grow old waiting for things to happen here.

It's not the same for their parents – that generation of West Indians who came over in the 40s and the 50s. They were encouraged to come here, like Willie Boy in *Playing Away*. They thought life was going to be great, they worked hard but today they still feel outside the gates of society and many of them question what they are doing here and want to go home to the Caribbean. I've lived in two worlds ever since I've been here.

I've made many documentaries. One that meant a lot to me was the recent one on Bhopal. I was sititng watching television with my family and this shocking event came on the news. I thought to myself, this could happen here, but how many people watching this in Britain would feel that? To them it would just be India, another disaster, peasants again. A few thousand of them die – so what? When I got to India, I found a culture thousands of years older than this one. I tried to deal with the human side of the disaster; what happened that night and how it affected them. All the news did was to deal with the legal and political implications and whether the Americans were going to pay up.

Making fiction feature films is very important to me as well because it can bring you closer to the emotions of the characters. You feel as if you are in their sitting-room with them. But I found some of the reactions to *Playing Away* very strange. Some reviews, especially in the hip, trendy, lefty magazines, criticised the representation of the white characters. Barry Norman said on television that 'Horace Ové is black and he knows about black people but he does not know about white people'. But I researched the film very carefully and these people do exist, and what is more they run the country. You only have to watch the House of Lords on television to know that this is true.

One of my future projects is an adaptation of James Baldwin's *Giovanni's Room*. He broke new ground with that novel since he is a black writer and there are no black characters in it. It will also probably be the first time a black director has made a film just about white people. It will be fascinating to see the reactions.

Reprinted with kind permission from *Monthly Film Bulletin*, v 54 n647, December 1987.

The Passion of Remembrance: Background

Martina Attille: Sankofa

In 1983, Sankofa applied to the Greater London Council Police Support Unit for money to make a 30-minute videotape documentary about policing in London. It was to be an historical account of the experiences of black people and policing in Britain. Isaac Julien, one of the members of the Collective, had produced *Who Killed Colin Roach?* (1983), a videotape focusing on the massive campaign that followed the mysterious death of Colin Roach in a North London police station. We thought we needed to produce a follow-up programme that put the Colin Roach death into a broader cultural and political context, to show some of the reasons for the mutual suspicion and distrust that exists between black communities and the police.

However, as we developed our ideas during the research and talked to various people, it became apparent that policing in its obvious sense was not the main issue, that there were more sailent forces at work which needed to be addressed instead; forces controlling the way we, as young black people, chose to express our lives and concerns. We decided to explore these other forms of control – our working title, 'Systems of Control', aptly conveyed our intentions, although we eventually dropped this title because it had lost its relevance as an indication of what was actually going on in the film.

complement the work of reappraisal, re-inscribing the black subject with a different set of values.

The varied responses to *Territories* and the discussions of 'Power/Control' all fed into the conception of *The Passion of Remembrance*. By Spring 1985, we had a clear idea of the direction we wanted to take the production. We approached Channel 4 Television (they had taken on the part-funding of several black workshops, including Sankofa, the previous year), to let them know that we now intended to do the film as a feature-length drama. This was all happening at a time when we were also getting more involved with film-makers from abroad, and realising the limitations of a documentary in an international context.

A drama fiction seemed an appropriate way to draw people into a film designed to be pleasurable and at the same time unapologetically political. We wanted the film to appeal to young black people, the politically aware and those who could become politically aware, a film for Europe about being young and black in Britain at a time of uncertainty. We also wanted the film to retain its original integrity – eg, the realities of policing in its broadest sense – and to assert the politics of being a black woman, always *active* (though people still insist on seeing us as 'emerging'), the racism/sexism that

Territories Isaac Julien

In late Autumn of 1984, we had organised a series of screenings and discussions under the heading, 'Power/Control', which was part of our research process. This confirmed what was already clear to us – namely, that despite the diversity of black life in Britain, images of black people are defined in a very narrow terms and contained as problematic, policing being a predictable arena. Our earlier film, *Territories* (1984/85) had already begun to talk about the way black cultures were being contained, while at the same time experimenting with a form that would

prevents us from being seen as taking the lead. Black women writers were becoming fashionable, but they were always important for us: they have traditionally written in the cracks paved over by popular movements, directly or indirectly in literature/publishing, in the black movements, in the feminist movements.

Maureen Blackwood and Isaac Julien pieced together our fragmented research, and developed a script with a mosaic quality that expressed the many things we wanted other people to experience. There was a sense of urgency to say it all, or at least to signal as much as we could in one film. Sometimes one can't afford to hold anything back for another time, or another conversation, or another film. That is the reality of our experience – sometimes we only get one chance to make ourselves heard.

When we started to develop the drama, there were some things that we felt were important in terms of our own history as part of the black communities: that there should be an unproblematised black family environment; that there should be no victims or heroes, but instead characters that work as a unity towards giving an impression of a total experience, where 'the generation gap' is less of a problem than people's resistance to change and new ideas. The lead characters had to be black women (and not your traditional 'tart') and we wanted them to have the edge, especially the Female Speaker (Anni Domingo).

The Female Speaker addresses the audience directly in the telling of her story. Her tone can be interpreted as arrogant, even condescending – she claims a superiority that you either rally behind or resent, depending on your own position in the power relations. Her character aims to interrupt the popular memory of a political past, a romantic memory as embodied by the Male Speaker (Joseph Charles) and Tony (Jim Findley). The old rhetoric seems somehow out of place in their anonymous landscape. The Female Speaker is intended to make us think again about the rhetoric of that 'sacred' past (not all of it can help us to prepare for the future, even though much of what was expressed then undoubtedly has resonance now).

The Speakers' Drama aimed to give an impression of what might be said by two people with differing experiences of 'the good old days' , of the 'real struggle'. Sankofa's particular character in terms of race, gender and sexualilty meant that the unfinished business of the 1960s/70s (black, gay and feminist movements) was something that we felt needed prioritising in the present, particularly in relation to those three areas of experience. The Speakers' interaction reworked the issues of a 'sacred' political past with the tensions we feel in the present.

We created the anonymous landscape and the interaction within it as a means of conveying what might happen in a situation where people got a chance to say what they really felt, at a time when maybe other issues took priority. In this case, the issues that couldn't quite make the political agenda seemed to be sexuality and gender. The language is sometimes irreverent, sometimes polemical. The anonymous space is intended to get away from the everyday in terms of language and appearance, it is an open environment that is overtly political – in contrast to the confinement of the city spaces in Maggie's (Antonia Thomas) world, where there's usually not enough time to think/debate, only time to react.

Of course, we also wanted the film to look good, to be shot well and to have spaces for humour and pleasure, so we tried to make it as interesting as possible as a filmic experience. We developed the structure to allow all the things we wanted to say to happen at the same time – like a soap opera, where you can go from one day to the next in the narrative without having to plant huge sign-posts. Thus, we change tenses without much warning in the narrative, but in the end it doesn't really matter because the issues are what hold the film together, and they can co-exist within that structure.

In both spaces in the film. 'The Speakers' Drama' and 'Maggie's Drama', we are saying similar things. However, the difference in approach between the two allows audiences a choice of entry points: some people can get into the more naturalistic elements, while others may prefer what's going on in the landscape. The film, nevertheless, intends to give an impression of a total experience, wherein there are fragments of that experience that we thought other people might share.

Maggie's space is important because there are so few images of young black people on the screen. We wanted contemporary images that looked appealing – black youth enjoying each other's company, having a laugh, having a dance, but knowing when to stop . . . for the serious times: Images that stay on the screen to do more than break-dancing, or chucking bricks through shop windows, as in typical riot news reports. For us, it is significant that Maggie and her friend, Louise (Janet Palmer) wear their lipstick and still claim to be politically conscious – it's a myth that feminism and lipstick are incompatible. We wanted to make a statement about pleasure, and about women's culture. Similarly, the boyfriends, Gary (Carlton Chance) and Michael (Gary McDonald) are 'real men' who kiss each other with a smack so loud that the pleasure in that intimacy cannot be denied.

Maggie's character is one that asks questions. She is trying to make sense of her environment, which has changed since the days of her parents, Gloria (Sheila Mitchell) and Benjy (Ram John Holder), or even of her elder brother, Tony – an England mapped by the film's locations and remapped by the archival footage (Maggie's videotape). The video material in the film is intended to document periods of recent British history, moments of celebration as well as protest, that will probably get lost in the retelling of popular history. It was important to document the visibility of public protest/demonstration, particularly at a time when those forms of public protest are increasingly threatened by public order legislation. Maggie's tape, the archival material, is also the backdrop for her 'confusion', in the sense that it signifies past definitions of struggle 'fighting back'.

The Passion of Remembrance attempts to take images of black people, and black independent production generally, out of the margins and prejudices constructed around 'minority' politics. It aims to look appealing and the themes are intended as universal. The film documents one dimension of a black experience, an experience of a political and aesthetic history, as well as the necessity for changes in the future.

Interview with
Sankofa Film Collective

**Martine Attille, Maureen Blackwood,
Nadine Marsh-Edwards and Isaac Julien in
dialogue with Jim Pines**

JP *The Passion of Remembrance* is concerned with the idea of reconstructing the historical past, ie, the notion of a reconstructed black political history, which in a sense offers a critique of historical moments in black people's struggle. But as the film's title suggests, the relationship with this past is an uneasy one – a mixture of respect, exhilaration and angst. Contrary to standard ethnic relations models, which tend to view the first generation of black people in Britain disparagingly, your narrative suggests a much more positive representation of their presence here, and it also suggests potential linkages that cut across generations, for example, within black family histories.

MB A lot has to do with how we are personally, as individuals who have made the film what it is. It's not that we haven't experienced history as a problem, but what we've always tried to do is actually to make sense of it. For example, my father was quite old when he died, and when I talked to him about his life, it was obvious that he was always trying to make sense of what had happened to him and what he had seen, how he had experienced things, and why he had experienced them in the way that he did – but that was only something he had done in later life.

So I think in trying to work out how you got where you are, you necessarily had to back-track in terms of finding out what had happened, what sets of circumstances got your parents to leave where they were to come here, what the nature of your family was, or is, or might be. I remember when I was at school and the teachers would be giving us one kind of history (conquests and discoveries), and then we would go home where our parents would give us another type of history (what hapened when and where) and we would always be asking ourselves: 'Do these two things meet up? No, they don't . . . sometimes they are different world views. So why is that, then? How do those things come about, and how do you actually position yourself within it?'

NME For me, the real turning point was when we met people who had helped to make the history of the 60s and 70s. They were figures of myth, we had read about them and in a sense looked up to them, because they had been fighting lots of battles on our behalf, whether we knew it or not. And it was sad the way they turned round and viewed us. Instead of looking at us as the next generation who could maybe carry on some of their work, they were trying to keep the history that they had created for themselves. It felt to me quite static and didn't envisage how the future could be changed. It was very strange to realise that we were a threat to people whom in fact we only had ever looked up to. I think everything kind of clashed together at a very similar time, when we were realising a lot of things about our position in this society as black women and as cultural practitioners.

IJ Yes, that was the big turning point, because after that it was really important for us to speak about the different versions of history, or regimes of truth, and to uncover the parameters of those different truths. It was almost like we had come into being, we were here, and yet they didn't understand why we were here. A lot of the dialogue in the film is about filling in those gaps in communication, first of all, by redefining our identities in Britain in terms of being young and black, and then redefining the specificities of that experience in terms of gender and sexuality.

It therefore became important for us to address the fact that we belong to different communities – ie, there isn't a homogeneous or monolithic black community, but rather different communities which together constitute the total black experience. So it was important to look at how we relate to each other positively, and not be oppressed by a hegemonic political discourse which says, for example, that there is only one way you are supposed to behave if you are a young black male. This is necessary not only in terms of political change, but also in terms of lifting the constraints that have been imposed on us, historically, by multi-culturalism or anti-racism, ie, the whole race relations paradigm.

MA I think the crucial dialectic in the film centres on the idea of public spaces and private spaces. There is an official history which somehow is the public space, where the official guardians of history, the self-appointed spokespeople in any given era, are allowed to give their version of the way things are. But beneath that, there is a private space where people actually live and experience the way things are. I think that in terms of the mythologised histories and the passion of that remembrance, we are a generation that is close enough to see what happened then in relation to what is happening now. But we were aware very early on that we weren't presenting any solutions. Rather, we see the film as an enquiry into how a political activist was defined in the past, and maybe how in the future we could construct ourselves in relation to race, class and sexuality.

JP Implicit in your notion of a reconstructed black political history, is the idea of different kinds of political consciousness informing black people's struggle. In other words, your emphasis on the diversity of black experiences serves to foreground the importance of 'private spaces', ie, the different strategies which individual black people have had to adopt in order to cope with their everyday situations.

MA Even though there are spokespeople taken up by institutions, or elected by a particular group, it doesn't mean that they are necessarily known by everyday people like our parents. So the question is, for example, how did the generation of the 50s survive? – because they didn't really get involved in popular movements or Black Power militancy. In fact, there were other ways of surviving, which often involved claiming some sort of invisibility, where you have a veneer which makes it appear as if everything is alright. But when you get down to it, what happened was your parents didn't go out, they didn't really get involved, they didn't get into trouble. That's not to say that they were naively thinking everything is okay, because they were well aware that the state is agressive towards them, but they had their own way of actually dealing with that. It's implicit in the way they behave and in their attitude to the wider white society: they had to make certain demands on themselves, it might not have been getting up on platform and making big speeches, but they did have to make demands in their personal relationships, on other people, on their workmates, etc. All of that is important for us in terms of reclaiming that legitimacy, that sort of experience.

JP The vignettes of family life in *The Passion* are particularly effective; the image you construct of black family life is very 'positive', which is in sharp contrast to conventional (race relations orientated) representations which usually stress notions of black family 'pathologies' and crisis. If there is a crisis (if one can call it that), you at least explore it without undermining the essential integrity of the black family.

MA We wouldn't deny that there is a crisis, but there have been different crises for us which appear in different ways. Our concern was to locate a black family in the 80s, and to have the different generations – Maggie, her elder brother, Tony, their mother and father – actually cohabiting and bringing their different experiences to that space. We didn't want to show them battling each other, but to place their experiences in a wider context. So we see Benjy, the father, for example, and the whole reference to him being unemployed, next to shots of the cityscape: he had contributed to all that build-up of wealth in this country and now he is unemployed. And then there are the youth who aren't yet unemployed. At the same time, we wanted to show that we don't go round with dark clouds over our backs every minute, that there is room for pleasure within that as well. So even though Benjy is unemployed, he is still able to relax and enjoy himself.

NME It was also important to show that, for black people, the family has been a main source of strength, it has been an area where you actually think you can survive living here. It's good to show that because the left, especially white feminists, like to attack the family as the area where you get most oppressed.

JP Can you say something about the anonymous landscape where the two speakers meet, and how this connects with your idea of public and private 'spaces'?

MA The idea was inspired by Ralph Ellison's *The Invisible Man*, where the central character is underground and the whole story is told from his position there. He is divorced from what is going on outside, but when the plot changes to have him actually meeting a woman, she is in the open space, which suggests possibilities. Female roles have to take on possibilities, because it is all about areas that are unfamiliar, like female sexuality. So the idea of 'space' became very important for us from the beginning. Although the Male Speaker meets the Female Speaker in an open space, we wanted him to be contained by another space, a mental or psychic space, in terms of his own political position. That's why he is in darkness when you first see him, and even though there is an interaction between them, he is still trapped in a kind of tunnel.

JP The implication is that he has lost his way politically, historically, intellectually; and that the woman – who was perhaps oppressed by the male 'leaders' within the movement, or at least wasn't given the kind of positive profile that she and other women in the struggle deserve – she has had the time to reflect

since then and is now able to say something substantive about where we are today.

MB It's a mixture of things. First of all, it has to do with different types of reflections of one situation. It also has to do with who has the power at any given time to make sense of those reflections in a public way. So you have a situation where people who rise to a certain station, or who are seen to be in the spotlight, they can actually give credence to a particular way of seeing, whereas people who have to take a back seat are not really in that position of power. In essence, what happens in the landscape is almost a kind of reversal process, but not exactly, because even though she is on her own turf and has that prominent position, she still allows space for the man to give his viewpoint, although she always has the upper hand.

From my perspective of writing it, she didn't come across as arrogant just from the written page. But when those words were spoken they were much more powerful and resonant. The actress, Anni Domingo, brought a lot of life to the words – just the look of her, the feel of her, she has an aura about her which I think brought a lot to the role and brought home a lot of the issues much more forcefully. So her 'arrogance' isn't something that I worry about in all, in fact, it's something that I think is quite pleasureable because it's very rare to see a black woman who is not frightened to say, 'This is what I think and you have to listen, you can't go away . . . I've waited too long for you to think that you have the power to walk away from me this time, because you are powerless in this situation in terms of direction; so you have to stay here and we have to talk about those things . . .' This doesn't mean that conversation has to be an equal one. The man brings his own point of view, and even though it is weaker than hers, it is weaker because what can you say in your own defence when you are actually guilty of never having listened to anyone else, when you have never given time for other sets of concerns? Those are the things we were thinking around.

MB We wanted to address the way in which at certain times particular issues are put high on the agenda. Historically, those issues have been around race and how black people are treated, employment, class, etc. Consequently, other equally important issues have tended to get left behind, for example, thoughts around sexuality, black women's position within the structure of black political organisations, and so on: they have had to take a back seat because there were thought to be more urgent things that needed addressing. In a sense, politics in the 80s is much more about trying to bring these other concerns forward, and to grapple with all of those issues at once, instead of saying, 'Well, let's just deal with class.' I think the film brings that home much more, I hope, to black communities, because obviously it is a film that is rooted within black communities.

When you look at the film, you are introduced to the characters: all you know about them is that they are black, you don't know what their political leanings are, you don't know anything about them, all you simply see is that they are black – but practically everybody in the film is black, so that is not an issue anymore. You are then forced to deal

with the interaction between everybody in the film, what's happening to them, what they choose to talk about, what they are, or what they hint at being, etc. And through that, we wanted to talk about black people's or black communities' responses to the visibility of gayness. We wanted to actually put our responses to that expression of emotion and love on the agenda as well, and actually to say 'Well, these characters are gay, what's your response? They haven't got a problem with it, so what's your problem with it?' -ie, to actually get people to start talking about homophobia and those types of issues.

The Passion of Remembrance Sankofa Film Collective

IJ Sexuality and gender are not usually included within a black political discourse, There has been a kind of cultural nationalist politics that says you can only talk about blackness and class. Those are the things that we are supposed to talk about first, with silences around questions of sexuality and gender. This has also been the whole way that white society has looked at the black subject, as being 'other'. But I think the really important issue has been around pleasure, and showing representations of experiences that have been invisible. The scene where Gary and Michael kiss is an example. Of course, we're not saying that kissing is political, although it's almost that in the sense that symbolically it is intended to confront certain issues. In fact, it is talking to minority audiences within the black communities, and it's also saying that this exists, that it happens. I think that if there's not a politics that can talk about the multiple differences and complexities within cultural differences, then there will be a real crisis.

MB There were certain things that we knew we wanted to put in the film, and through a process of different drafts we came to roughly what we have. We shot the film near enough to what was on paper, so the way it looks, dramatically, corresponds closely to what was written. It wasn't really a question of wanting to make a certain kind of film, but rather deciding on the sets of concerns that we wanted to get across, and within the writing and rewriting, working out the best way to put those things forward.

MA And this includes an economic reality as well, in terms of budget, how much you can actually do, etc. Financing the film was not easy and the budget was always too low for what we wanted to achieve. For example, we wanted to develop a fuller sense of characters and relationships within the family but that in the end didn't materialise. So it's not just a purely artistic or formal exercise to produce a film like *The Passion*. You are working within given economic realities as well.

MA We were always conscious of our audiences and whether people would be able to make sense of the narrative. We went through the whole process of inviting people in to see the rough cuts, to get their responses and to see how different sets of people would actually make sense of the film. They did, by and large, make sense of it, and were able actually to get quite a lot from the film, even with its supposedly abstract kind of form.

IJ The starting point for us was what we were trying to say, as Maureen said, and the text being important. And that text was related to different constituencies, different audiences of interest. I think that is what will draw people's interest, because there are not many films that have black women in major roles, and there are no films that will have black gays featured in them. I think people will want to come to see those things because, hopefully, there are identifications on offer. They are not invisible, those audiences, they are a kind of silent majority.

MA It's not so much targeting in different parts of the film, or targetting specific audiences. I think it's more to do with working with an assumption about what is available to audiences as a whole. Audiences are visually sophisticated and have been exposed to, and are open to, lots of different forms. Perhaps because we are the first generation that has grown up on television: it has affected our pacing, the way we switch from channel to channel, with all those different things happening at different times, and yet we can still make sense of it all. So it's like working with an assumption that people can make sense of things pretty quickly, and also that our experience is not a marginal one – we are very much part of a mainstream, we actually draw on influences from across the board, not just within the ethnic minorities slot, or the women's slot, or the gay slot.

Reprinted with kind permission from *Framework* in 32/33 1986.

Ceddo:
The Peoples' Account

Our Right to make Valid Critical Comment

The People's Account has effectively been banned by the IBA, unless we, the programme makers, agree to make 'small' editorial cuts. Clearly Mr Glencross wants us to forget our rights as programme makers to make valid and critical comments. In his apparently unchallengeable position, he feels able to impose his moral and political judgements not only on us but on everybody. His discretion seems final on what is acceptable for transmission.

In his view, *The People's Account* is 'an angry and one-sided film'. He has even gone as far as describing the commentary on the police as 'racist', failing to understand that racism stems from and is perpetrated by an authoritative system which those in power direct to their advantage. In our view, the film gives a black people's perspective and we did not feel it necessary to engage in liberal 'balancing' of views. The film itself balances much of the hysterical media bias which greeted the uprisings and it reflects the views of numerous women, men, the youth and elders of community.

The struggle to transmit *The People's Account* is a contest of truth over control. The truthful representation and interpretation of black people's experience is just one part of it; there are many other truths which need to be told.

Sandra Eccleston
of Ceddo Film and Video Workshop,
based in Tottenham, North London.

Open Letter to Mr Glencross

Director of Television, IBA
Dear Mr Glencross
Re: *The People's Account* and political censorship

My attention has been drawn to what, on the face of the matter, is your proposed censorship of the film, *The People's Account*, made last year by the Ceddo Film and Video Workshop. Ceddo, as you will know, is a collective of black film-makers.

Your act of evident censorship consists of your demand that three specific phrases used in the film be excised before it can be shown on Channel 4 – and presumably any other part of the Independent Television network.

I write both as the author of two of the phrases you wish to censor and as a member of one of Britain's black communities. I hope it is common ground between us that the three phrases at issue would not, if broadcast either singly or together, break any law. What is at stake, therefore, is in the first instance your interpretations of your statutory rights over what is permissible for broadcasting on the TV network.

The People's Account presents a view from within the black communities of the consequences in the domain of public order of the persistently lawless – not yet to say racist – policing we experience. This is a matter which is ignored or misunderstood at the peril of us all. How do acts of censorship of the sort you contemplate aid understanding? You are surely not intending it to be understood that a self-proclaimed liberal media will not allow black people's experiences of life – including policing – in the UK to be talked about by us within the law

without censorship? If so, we are going to have increasing difficulty spotting the difference between liberal and fascist media.

The further question must be asked: is your statutory duty being exercised in an even-handed and non-racist way where the broadcasting of material relating to the black communities is concerned? Perhaps you will be able to recall for the benefit of members of these communities when the IBA last did something to prevent/mitigate the steady stream of racist TV programming – directly insulting as well as threatening to the well-being of black people settled here – broadcast on radio and TV channels covered by your statutory responsibility. It would be tedious to cite the documentation upon which this assertion rests. However, if you take issue with it, I shall be happy to do so. Why is it that you appear to do so little against racist programming? Is it because it offends only black people and anti-racists? Why, by contrast, your detail interest in this small video by Ceddo? Does that interest derive from the fact that the black people who made it raise some wholly legal questions about societal racism and, more particularly, about the racialism of that scared institution, the police?

May I comment briefly on the particular phrases you say must be deleted before *The People's Account* can be beamed into the homes of our white and black fellow citizens.

The description of Mrs Cherry Groce as 'a victim of police racism'. You may well be among those who take the view (based on a particular stipulation of the meaning of racism) that, since British police forces are self-evidently not racist, there can be no victims of their racism. If so, nothing will persuade you of the validity of holding that a black woman shot down in her own home by a policeman who regarded her as no more than a menacing 'dark shadow' can be called a victim of police racism.

Alternatively you may be of the opinion that, since most of those recently shot 'in error' and 'in self defence' by policemen in England are white (these include a sleeping boy of five and a pregnant woman as well as Stephen Waldorf), the shooting of a black woman cannot be 'racist'. Indeed, it could even be seen as an anti-racist attempt by the good Inspector Lovelock to include us in an area of national life from which – the case of Colin Roach notwithstanding – we had previously been excluded. If this is the argument on which you are relying for the censorship of the phrase concerning Mrs Groce, I invite you to take account of the fact that what Mrs Groce is suffering fits not only into the pattern of shootings just mentioned. It also fits into a pattern of police violence towards members of the black communities, which has traumatised and angered individuals, familes, and black communities both locally and nationally. This pattern unwinds into a long history of police practices towards our communities, which we rationally interpret as racialism not unconnected to police and broader societal racism. Here also I refrain from citing the considerable body of writing which at least begins to document and speak of this history: but, of course, I should gladly do so if, indeed, you are disposed to dispute the matter.

In the light of the pattern of police violence towards black people, into which we in the black communities placed what happened to Mrs Groce, I find it incredible that you have discovered any laws, facts or tastes which render it wrong for *The People's Account* to refer to Mrs Groce as 'a victim of police racism'. Why do you wish to censor this phrase? I am sure you are a person of considerable imagination as a Director of Television for the IBA. This may be why you can envisage an armed police officer bursting into a Hampstead home in search of a person known to be white, failing totally to check out either the layout or the occupancy of the house, and then shooting down the white mother of the house as, in panic, she rushes from her bedroom, becoming a meanacing 'fair shape' in the process. Why can it not be said in a film commentary on Channel 4 that racism, much more than any of the other fanciful factors, is what made it possible for such a thing to happen in Brixton with Cherry Groce – a black mother – as victim.

The phrase *'police terror raids continue'*. It may well be that the IBA has an unbreachable rule that the word 'terror' can never be used in respect of any conceivable action by British police forces. If so, what appears in this instance as censorship is in reality merely your way of securing compliance. One would hope that such rules could be notified in advance to film-makers.

If no such rule is in operation, the key issue becomes the accuracy of this phrase as used in a descriptive caption in *The People's Account*. Ceddo uses the phrase in the context of the presentation of direct evidence from Broadwater Farm residents of the ways in which police behaviour there, in the aftermath of the disturbances of late 1985, put them in terror. There is neither mystery nor mystique about this word: reliance is placed on the *Oxford English Dictionary*'s definition of it as 'the state of being terrified or greatly frightened; intense fear, fright or dread'.

The residents in question – young black mothers – testified to being terrorised by Metropolitan Police raids in which officers armed with guns and sledge hammers, and uttering the most vile racial abuse, entered their homes in the early hours of the morning. Not all the evidence of this sort which Ceddo had at its disposal could be deployed in the video. A great deal more evidence of this sort was made available to the Broadwater Farm Inquiry chaired by Lord Gifford.

If black people living on the Broadwater Farm Estate were in fact put in terror by the Metropolitan Police, why exactly does the IBA wish to censor a caption which acknowledges this?

The description of the disturbances at Broadwater Farm as *'a classic example of self-defence by a community'*. It seems, at first glance, a difficult phrase to justify: a phrase waiting for the blue pencil, as it were. It is therefore important to understand the contexts in which it is used in *The People's Account*. Be assured, first, that its use is neither trivial nor deliberately provocative.

Self defence is not an easy notion. It is applied very strictly in *The People's Account* to the justified response of people put in fear by the threat and actuality of illegal physical force. There is evidence from the magistrates court hearing of the case against Floyd Jarrett, from the inquest into the death of his mother Mrs Cynthia Jarrett, from the previously mentioned Gifford Inquiry into the Broadwater Farm disturbances and elsewhere, that those disturbances took place at the end of a long train of illegal acts by members – in growing numbers – of the Metropolitan Police. These include (a) the wrongful arrest and false charging of Floyd Jarrett, (b) the illegal use of keys to gain entry to his mother's house, (c) the obtaining of a search warrant for the search of that house no earlier than during or after it and (d) manhandling of Mrs Jarrett thus contributing to her death.

But the most important illegal act by police officers on the day was (e), their move to prevent a lawful and peaceable demonstration from going on its way from the Broadwater Farm Estate to the local police station. I know of no explanation as to why the Metropolitan Police sent a squad of riot-equipped officers to prevent that demonstration by seeking physically to confine those wishing to take part to the Estate. This action by the police was certainly of dubious legality. In the ensuing clash, the police were the agressors against persons acting defensively. If the police had allowed matters to rest there, or pursued those they thought offenders over a more protracted time-scale, the real tragedies of the Broadwater Farm disturbances (which include the death of police constable Keith Blakelock, no less than the mishandling of those charged with his murder from start to finish, and the terrorising effects of the extended police follow-up operation) would never have occurred. This is not a trivial point.

It is a pity that the Metropolitan Police learn so selectively from Lord Scarman. They learned and applied his dictum about 'sterile areas', put forward following the Red Lion Square disturbances, in Southall in 1979 with deliberate and devastating effect. What they did not learn and apply at Broadwater Farm is Scarman's dictum – a re-emphasis of Kerner – that in civil disturbances it is wise to leave people an escape route.

By seeking to follow up the initial clash with demonstrators at one of the entrances to the Broadwater Farm Estate with an entry onto the estate with a larger and ever more menacing force, the Metropolitan Police obliged those on the estate to defend it against them. The view of the commentary of *The People's Account*, reflecting a widely held view in the black community, is that these whom the police confined to the Broadwater Farm Estate on that afternoon were forced to defend themselves, which they did with such signal success as to justify the phrase 'a classic example of self defence by a community'. It was self-defence *against police illegality and error.*

Yours sincerely,
Cecil Gutzmore,
Commentary Writer
The People's Account

Reprinted with kind permission from Kwesi Owusu, ed, *Storms of the Heart: An Anthology of Black Arts and Culture,* Camden Press, 1988.

An Interview with Black Audio Film Collective

John Akomfrah, Reece Auguiste, Lina Gopaul and Avril Johnson in dialogue with Coco Fusco

CF I would like to get a sense of what ideas, what arguments were being debated at the time that you all began to work.

LG I'll just open by saying that there was always a sense of the lines we didn't want to pursue, lines which were more didactic. That the riots, for example, happened because of x y z, and that these are the reasons and these are the solutions for it – regardless of whether they were being thrown out by the Left, be it the white or the black Left. I think our coming together at that time was an expression of not wanting to take up one of those particular positions. And by choosing not to we threw ourselves into a field that was very grey. We then tried to pull out certain themes that we agreed with – what Stuart Hall might have been saying at that time, or what Paul Gilroy might have been saying.

JA But you're not just talking about making *Handsworth Songs* (1986) are you?

CF I'd like to go back further, prior to *Handsworth*.

LG Even before that our position was not one of which you could say that it takes its meaning from this or that.

CF It seems that there was a strong cultural nationalist position that was generated by the black activist community – and to some extent, the more conventionally oriented black media sectors. But speaking in terms of ideas, in terms of theorizing race and nationality, such activity was not coming out of those sectors.

RA They were the residues of the 1970s, of the Black Power movements that existed here, which did have a very strong nationalist slant. What motivated us was not wanting to rearticulate past political positions but rather to engage with broader theoretical issues which had not yet been addressed, or at least not in the way that we wanted to address them.

There were many discussions in the '70s and early'80s about the post-pan-Africanist vision, or the pan-Africanist vision. And a lot of that was, in many respects, undertheorized. So what we did was to combine, very critically, elements of those debates, drawing also on our own theoretical background which we had developed at colleges. We are in many respects a kind of hybrid: we are able to draw from Foucauldian discourse, psychoanalysis, Afro-Caribbean discourse, and colonial and neocolonial narratives. I was going to signpost Jacques Lacan, but in many respects I think that Franz Fanon[1] would be closer to what I am communicating. *Expeditions* (1983), which was our first cultural project, was a way of testing those ideas and trying to extend the power of the images and debates around the colonial and postcolonial moment. In order to do that we had to articulate a particular language and vision of that moment. We felt we could only do so by drawing on those European, theoretical discourses.

JA If you look at the moment of becoming for the black film and video sector in this country, there are a number of words which were key. One of them obviously was representation. The other was more a category than a term: colonial discourse. The minute you begin to work out the political etymology of those terms themselves you are effectively charting the histories and trajectories of those individuals and collectivities.

The notion of representation had been projected into the forefront by a number of discussions in post-Althusserian circles. Different political currents in this country had an interest in it for different reasons. What was being debated was the value of a Left political culture and how one represents that culture in discourse theory. Gramscians had an interest in it because they had come to the conclusion that political power and cultural symbolic power were organized around consent. In terms of a black interest – on one level a number of collectives, including ourselves, were familiar with the semiologic activities of Parisian intellectuals. So all those currents inform how the collective was set up. Four years ago in England you couldn't sit through a discussion, a film meeting, without representation coming up about fifteen million times.

LG It goes further too than the issue of representation. We were involved, in doing work with *Expeditions*, in an attempt to put another phrase or category on the political agenda – colonial discourse. It wasn't being discussed everywhere, – mostly in particular academic circles. And what we wanted to do was to address those debates, those theories, and to bring them onto a visual landscape.

JA People use the term representation for a number of reasons. The different uses give you a sense of the complexity of the trajectories involved. At one level people used it to simply talk about questions of figuration. How one places the black in the scene of writing, the imagination and so on. Others saw it in more juridic terms. How one is enfranchised, if you like, how one buys into the social contract. What is England and what constitutes English social life? Some interests were broadly academic, but we were focussing on how to turn our concerns into a problematic, to use an Althusserian term, in the cultural field. We were interested in representation because it seemed to be partly a way of prying open a negative/positive dichotomy. It seemed to be a way of being able to bypass certain binaries.

CF Are you referring now to the negative and positive image debates?

JA Yes, and their specifically English variant – which is obsessed with stereotypes, with grounding every discussion around figuration in cinema in terms of stereotyping. It as a way of going beyond the discussions which would start at the level of the stereotype, then move on to images, and then split images into negative and positive, and so on. We wanted to find a way to bypass this, without confronting it head on. I think that the lobbies which were really interested in debates around stereotyping were too strong, to be honest. And we were too small to take them head on. In a sense the negative/positive image lobby represented all that was acceptable about anti-racism, multiculturalism, etc. It's the only thing that united everybody who claimed they were against racism.

Post-Colonial Memory

RA The positive/negative image discourse had become the organizing principle of what representation was supposed to have been about, what representation was. *Expeditions* was an attempt to critique that discourse on positive and negative images. We wanted to go beyond purely descriptive categories and then to forge another kind of analytical strain, which could then open up that space in which we could begin to articulate our own ideas about representation by problematizing representation itself.

When *Expeditions* was first completed we had a number of theoretical, political and cultural battles with those who had very defined ideas about what representation was. The first point that was made was that it was inaccessible, because we were using language which was grounded in Foucauldian ideas, and Fanonian ideas, and so on. Second, there was the issue of the kind of images we used, which had not been used before. The way, for example, in which we would actually appropriate from English national fictions – like the Albert and Victoria Memorial – going back and really engaging with the archive of colonial memory. We were not only constructing a colonial narrative, but also critiquing what was seen as the colonial moment – critiquing what was seen as the discourse around empire.

CF One of the desires of postmodernism in its most Eurocentric form is to sever the tie between the political implication and the formal manifestation. In *Expeditions* you use similar strategies of appropriation with a different objective. Do you see these as two postmodernisms hitting off one another? Were you misread because of this?

RA One of the problems of the discourse of postmodernity lies in what it excludes. The crisis that the postmodern is supposed to address is seen as something internal to the logic and the rationale of Western Classical Civilization. In philosophical discourse there is the crisis around reason. Then there is a crisis around form, as manifested in architecture. What interests me most about these debates is the exclusion of the so-called neocolonial world. To me the crisis doesn't have so much to do with what's happening to the West, to the internal discourse of the West, as it does with what the non-European world is doing to the West. The crisis now is in Lebanon, in South Africa.

JA In terms of the beginning of making *Expeditions*, it's important to say that there are two convergences there. On the one hand, we realized that there was a kind of reappropriation, which we now understand to be postmodernist reappropriation of the past, taking place in very formalist circles, such as the kind of work that Victor Burgin and others were doing in photography. What we decided to do – which again, with hindsight, we now realize places us firmly in that camp – was to appropriate classical or neoclassical images. But we appropriated them using methods of avant-garde photography which effectivly begin with Alexander Rodchenko[2] – extremely angular kinds of framing, etc. That was the key difference. If you look at the formalist work on the other hand, the methods of composition

were extremely straightforward. Henri Cartier Bresson[3] could have done it. What people found unnerving about what we were doing was that the play of postmodernism wasn't there. *This* parody and pastiche was underpinned by biblical sounding tones concerning colonial narratives and expeditions and so on. We wanted to say that it was an exhibition, that on the one hand you went through these exhibitions – you pack your bag from different aesthetic fields, from neoclassical architecture, from Russian formalist photography. But the interest was in colonial narrative. The interest was not, in the end, in play.

Expeditions Black Audio Film Collective

Battle Zones

CF Let's move on to *Handsworth Songs*. I am interested in the symptomatic qualities of the responses to it. I do think that the fact *Handsworth Songs* has been the subject of controversy has to do with something larger than the film. It has to do with a desire to damage the kind of position you represent. Salman Rushdie's frequently mentioned review in *The Guardian* doesn't really address the film – he demonstrates no relationship to the filmic aspects of the work. He juxtaposes the notion of an authentic voice to image manipulation.

LG I think this goes back to what we were saying about where we located ourselves in relation to the political and theoretical positions that prevailed prior to our existence as a collective. When we emerged people tried to didactically map out the cultural and visual terrain for us to slot into.

If they were not actually addressing the film, well then what is it that they were addressing? Transgression, basically. Why were there such strong responses not to the film, but our existence? To what we represented? Those who criticized us most vehemently were prioritizing a line about community and people in the streets. There was no other way of representing ourselves other than the way they put forward.

JA The question of paternity and transgression was very important. One of the things which people would always say to us was, isn't *Handsworth Songs* too avant-garde? Quite simply, the problems we faced in making *Handsworth* were very practical ones – to do with melodrama – orchestrating means of identification, rather than distancing people and dazzling them with techniques. The editing might be considered unconventional, but the techniques are very straightforward. So it's not avant-garde in that sense. My mistake was in assuming people wouldn't see it as a transgressive text.

In terms of the established boundaries of discussion – aesthetic interventions around race – there were questions of paternity at stake. In other words, who was the holder of the law – the law of enunciation? who had the right to speak, who had the right to map out and broaden the field that everybody had to speak in? It was in that sense that the film was received as a transgressive text, because it clearly didn't fall into line with the established concordat concerning the black intelligensia and their discussion of race. That then makes the film an avant-garde text. Those who were willing to live with a more mixed economy of dialogue around figuration and race accepted it, and those who didn't, did not accept it.

LG It was also a move away from the specificity of location. After 1981, there was a generalized understanding of the riots, whereas in 1985 it was different. How can we begin to understand this situation, people would ask, in Birmingham, which didn't riot in 1981? Birmingham has a very specific black political history. It's one of the central spots for black political development and for anti-racist development. It has a number of institutions, like the Centre for Contemporary Cultural Studies, which are based within those communities. There is something quite specific happening there.

JA We have to be careful not to overestimate the transgressive potential of certain kinds of aesthetic intervention. At a certain point, the nightmares which weigh on the brain are not necessarily historical ones – they are very conjunctural ones. The fact of the matter is that a number of things were collapsing at a certain point. And the film in many ways mirrors that collapse. It's not an avant-gardist intervention, in the sense that it doesn't frame a series of devices that would get us out of the crisis. It mirrors those forms collapsing, and it says what a shame.

CF How did people respond to that sort of mirror?

JA When people saw the film they saw all the fractures, which are quite deliberate. Part of the problem that we have has to do with the question of whether black people should be involved in visual arts, in creating aesthetically challenging visual work. The assumption when we foreground avant-garde technique is either that we don't know anything else, and have stumbled across it by accident, or that we are imitating other forms.

LG Or that we have no foundation in the black communities, that we've left that behind too.

JA The idea of prefacing the film with a phrase – 'There are no stories in the riots, only the ghosts of other stories' – and then to work on it in terms of splits and unevenesses and so on without trying to centre it was what alarmed many people. The triumphalist vision of race and community operates on the assumption that there is essentially a core of affect that is structured around oratory, around song – giving it an irreducible unity – which wasn't present in the film. It played with it, at some stages discards it, it takes it on board, then it says it's probably not possible, do not work with it, but there you are, and so on. But the film doesn't fix its sentiments around it. That is what was frightening, and what led to the discussion of whether avant-garde techniques, or disruptive techniques, profilmic techniques, are in safe hands when they are given to blacks. Both certain black theorists and the white theorists would say that; they would want to know whether authorship is really safe with us.

1 Franz Fanon was born in Martinique, studied psychiatry in France and worked in Algeria during the Franco-Algerian War. He is the author of *Black Skin, White Masks, The Wretched of the Earth*, and *A dying Colonialism.*

2 Alexander Rodchenko, the Russian constructivist artist and photographer of the early revolutionary period.

3 Henri Cartier-Bresson, the French photographer and photojournalist.

Edited and Reprinted with kind permission from *Young, British and Black*, produced by Hallwalls Arts Centre, Buffalo, NY

ICA documents

Half way between the spoken and written word, this unique series of magazines engages with key intellectual and theoretical debates and provides a point of access to what is often difficult contemporary thinking. Contributors – all of whom have participated in ICA discussions – come from a diversity of disciplines. Applauded for their novel format, **ICA Documents** bring you leading thinkers, fresh perspectives, a forum for ideas on the page.

Desire
ICA Documents 1
Culture and the State
ICA Documents 2
Ideas from France
ICA Documents 3
Postmodernism
ICA Documents 4-5
Identity: The Real Me
ICA Documents 6
Black Film/ British Cinema
ICA Documents 7

Institute of Contemporary Arts
The Mall, London SW1 5AH

ISSUE SIX – OUT NOW!
THE GOOD VIDEO GUIDE

L ively, provocative and diverse, *New Formations* has already become a magnet for innovative cultural theory and debate from around the world. In its first year, *New Formations* published Ien Ang on progressive television, Georgina Born on musical postmodernism, David Edgar on drama and carnival, Dick Hebdige on the sublime, Elizabeth Cowie and Norman Bryson on Mary Kelly's *Interim*, Julia Kristeva on melancholy, Greil Marcus on subversive singers, Kobena Mercer on the politics of hair, Jacque Rancière on romantic travellers, Denise Riley on 'women', Alan Sinfield on English and modernism, Ginette Vincendeau on *chanteuses réalistes*, Peter Wollen on fashion and orientalism, and much more . . .

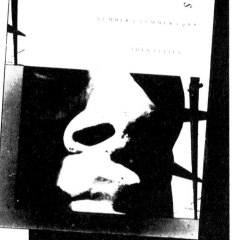

No wonder *City Limits* said "it looks set to become a vital tool in honing an awareness of the politics of culture. The range of writers and topics is impressive."

New Formations is published three times a year, in April, June and October. (ISSN 0950-2378)
Each issue 234x153mm, 144pp and illustrated.

	World (ex. USA & Canada)	USA & Canada
Institutions:	£38.50	Institutions: $63.00
Individuals:	£22.00	Individuals: $42.00

Subscription enquiries and sample copy requests to:

Michelle Swinge,
Routledge Promotion Dept.,
11 New Fetter Lane,
London EC4P 4EE.

4: Cultural Technologies

Includes Simon Frith on the British reception of Black American music, Griselda Pollock on Doré's London, Colin Mercer on entertainment, Tony Bennett on museums and exhibitions, and Ian Hunter setting limits to culture.

5: Identities

Homi Bhabha on theory's third way, Philip Cohen on racism, Glenn Bowman on Palestinian nationalism, Kristin Ross on Rimbaud, Kaja Silverman on the Statue of Liberty, Adrian Rifkin on *Carmen*, Margaret Soltan on *Vagabonde*, etc.

New Formations 6 (Winter 1988/9) features 'the Blues', and 1989 opens with a special issue on modernity.

Editor: James Donald

Reviews editor: Homi K Bhabha

R
Routledge